THE MULTI-PROBLEM FAMILY

A REVIEW
AND
ANNOTATED BIBLIOGRAPHY

THE MULTI-PROBLEM FAMILY

A Review and Annotated Bibliography

BENJAMIN SCHLESINGER

Editorial Consultant
FLORENCE STRAKHOVSKY

THIRD EDITION

UNIVERSITY OF TORONTO PRESS

© University of Toronto Press 1963

Second edition 1965

Third edition
© University of Toronto Press 1970

Printed in Canada
Reprinted in 2018
ISBN 0-8020-1726-6
ISBN 978-1-4875-8236-4 (paper)

To

CHARLES E. HENDRY

in affection and gratitude

THE LAIDLAW FOUNDATION

The primary interests of the Laidlaw Foundation lie in the fields of psychology, social welfare and sociology. The Directors believe that Foundation funds should be used to stimulate the development of new ideas and to experiment with new approaches to old problems. For this reason, grants are not made to supplement regular agency budgets. Capital grants are restricted to those associated with the development of a new and needed service.

The Directors were pleased to make a grant in support of the publication of this annotated bibliography of literature concerning multi-problem families. This grant complements the Foundation's support of a family-centred research project in London, Ontario. It is to be hoped that the knowledge gained through these projects may be helpful to others endeavouring to improve their community health and welfare services.

Publication of reports of work supported by a Foundation grant does not imply responsibility of the Foundation for the content of the work, or agreement with the opinions expressed: these are properly the responsibility of the authors.

PREFACE TO THIRD EDITION

Upon completion of the first edition of this annotated bibliography it was the author's intention to bring the material up to date by periodic supplements. The second edition partly met that hope, in that Appendix A included items dealing with multi-problem families from November 1962 to April 1965. In contrast to the wealth of items reported for the previous years, only fifteen items relating directly to multi-problem families were then reported.

Shortly after completion of the first edition, emphasis in social welfare shifted to the "War on Poverty". This was evident in the literature, where the focus of concern was on "poverty". That the multi-problem families can be considered to be the "very poor" emerged clearly at the UNESCO International Conference on Socially Handicapped Families held in Paris in February 1964 (see reference #316). An annotation of the literature on poverty was not attempted in the second edition but has since been compiled by the author and published (Poverty in Canada and the United States: Overview and Annotated Bibliography, Toronto: University of Toronto Press, 1966; reprinted 1968). Nor was the increasing literature on family-centred casework or therapy included, since quite a few publications review that area extensively.

Despite intensive effort and the wealth of studies on poverty, our multi-problem families are still very much with us. In this third edition an essay by the author has been added, which reviews Canadian efforts to date in an attempt to understand the persistence of this social phenomenon.

Please note that two items in the bibliography, #182 and #227, should have been listed under Britain rather than under United States.

B. S.

CONTENTS

Preface to Third Edition	vii
Introduction	xi
The Multi-Problem Family by John Spencer	3

Community Treatment Programs
   for Multi-Problem Families
      by Joseph C. Lagey and Beverly Ayres
	55

The Multi-Problem Family in Canada:
   A Glance Backward
      by Benjamin Schlesinger
	73

List of Abbreviations	88
Bibliography	
Australia	89
Britain	90
Canada	104
France	113
Holland	114
United States	117
Miscellaneous	169
Appendix A: Bibliography, December 1962- April 1965	174
List of Addresses	179
Author Index	187

INTRODUCTION

The compilation of an annotated bibliography on the multi-problem family can be likened to a detective investigation, which searches for clues, evidence, and witnesses. It all began at a small conference in Toronto, part of which was devoted to the multi-problem family. Someone in the group asked, "What is being done about such families in other parts of the country and world?" Everyone present looked puzzled and not a voice was raised in answer.

With the help of Professor Ray Godfrey, of the University of Toronto, School of Social Work, I developed a student group research project which dealt with multi-problem families. In my search for references I contacted Melbourne, London, Paris, The Hague, New York, St. Paul, and Vancouver. The next source of help came from twenty professional journals in five countries, which published my request for material for the present volume. Social work colleagues responded immediately, and daily the postman delivered items from far and wide. Along came personal letters of encouragement to proceed with such an annotation. And thus the book took shape, with the help of social workers, social agencies, community councils, journals, and government sources around the world. It is indeed a co-operative effort.

Dr. John Spencer, my colleague at the School of Social Work, has written a trend report of the multi-problem family, in an attempt to put into focus our knowledge in this important facet of social welfare. Since most of the annotations are from North America, I was fortunate to have as added contributors Miss Beverly Ayres and Dr. Joseph Lagey of the Community Chest and Councils of the Greater Vancouver Area. They are sharing with our readers their recent study of multi-problem family projects in American and Canadian communities.

The annotations are classified according to countries, and each country's items are arranged alphabetically by authors. A complete list of sources and publishers, to enable the reader to write for any specific item of interest, is included, as well as an author index. The items in the book were selected up to November 1, 1962. It is my hope that we can bring this bibliography up to date every few years, if the co-operation of our readers in sending relevant material to me continues as fervently as it began.

    The team which worked very hard to produce this volume included May Etkin, who did a lot of the background research, Florence Strakhovsky, whose editorial advice was invaluable, Sadie Gerridzen, who compiled the index, and Roselyn Glass, who typed the complete manuscript in its final form. The Director, Board, and Staff of the North York and Weston Family Service were helpful in discussing some of the material. I am also very grateful to Mary-Claire Thomas of the Laidlaw Foundation, who encouraged me in this endeavour, to the Laidlaw Foundation for the grant which made the undertaking possible, and to the Harry M. Cassidy Memorial Research Fund, which administered the grant.

B. S.

THE MULTI-PROBLEM FAMILY

A REVIEW
AND
ANNOTATED BIBLIOGRAPHY

THE MULTI-PROBLEM FAMILY

John C. Spencer

Families troubled by a multiplicity of problems are clearly not the concern of any one country; they are to be found everywhere. But there can be little doubt that higher standards of wealth and the high expectations of behaviour held by the social welfare services of Western society have brought to public attention a difficult and challenging social problem that previously has remained concealed. People feel both puzzled and angry and, above all, frightened by the exploitative behaviour of the nonconformist minority of families who take from society far more than they contribute, who fail to respond in any positive manner to the efforts of the social services to rehabilitate them, who appear to transmit the same patterns of behaviour from one generation to another, and whose disorganized and often destructive way of life seems to threaten society's basic values and standards.[1]

To say this is not to imply that public reaction to the multi-problem family is justifiable; it is merely to draw attention to some of the reasons for concern. In this Bibliography the literature is drawn predominantly from the United States, Great Britain, and Canada, but the "multi-problem family" (or "problem family", and "familles-problèmes" as it is also called) is easily recognizable in many other countries, particularly in those with high levels of living. This report is concerned with the internal behaviour of these families and their relationship with the social environment in which

---

I wish to acknowledge the invaluable help of Mrs. May Etkin not only in studying the literature but more especially in the initial preparation of this report. I am grateful also to my colleagues, Dr. T. Grygier, Professor John Morgan, and Miss Ruth Robinson, and to Mrs. Florence Strakhovsky for her helpful editorial and general advice.

they live, and it aims at assessing the development and nature of our present knowledge and at clarifying the lines of future study and practice.

The frequently used labels, "hard core" or "hard to reach", are in themselves indications of the multi-problem family's outstanding characteristic -- its resistance to existing methods of help and treatment. The question of multi-problem family study and treatment, however, should be related to the study and treatment of disordered and disorganized family behaviour in general.

I

Development of the Concept of Multi-Problem Family

The term "multi-problem family" in North America, and its counterpart "problem family" in Great Britain, both suffer from the weakness, that administrative categories generally have limited diagnostic value. "Problem" is in itself a vague concept. It is frequently used as an indication of the symptoms troubling a family rather than as a precise diagnostic label. There are few families in any society or social class which have no problems. But it is the nature and severity of the problems and the anxiety and hostility to which they give rise in society that appear to characterize the multi-problem families. Thus, the concept has sometimes proved to be an effective rallying point for social action on the part of the community.

Its history in Great Britain is characterized by the growing contrast with earlier times in standards of family living expected in a "Welfare State" and the inability of a minority to achieve the expected level. There can be little doubt that the multi-problem family was to be found among Charles Booth's "submerged tenth" at the turn of the century and among the "social problem group" of the Report of the Mental Deficiency (Wood) Committee in 1929.[2]

During the 19th century criminologists and social reformers were struck by the widespread and persistent criminality of certain social classes which they labelled "classes dangereuses" or "classes criminelles". But we have no reliable estimate of the extent to which these groups were similar in characteristics to the "multi-problem families". One thing is clear -- the multi-problem family becomes more noticeable as the standards of a society rise. Its chronic failure in the basic tasks of child rearing, household management, and earning a living stands out in sharp relief against a general improvement in family welfare.

The concept of the multi-problem family has developed specifically out of the family's inability to function adequately in its environment. Earlier students of the problem in Great Britain thought in terms of a "social problem group" rather than of specific families. The term "social problem group" was introduced by the Wood Committee to denote "an aggregate of families which, according to the findings of six comprehensive and well-planned enquiries, comprised a large proportion of high-grade defectives. The members of these mostly large families presented multiple social problems in addition to that of mental defect, which had provided the starting point of the enquiries." It was sub-normality of intelligence that was seen as the main factor contributing to the economic dependency of this group. During the last decade in Great Britain emphasis has shifted from the factor of intelligence towards factors of personality. Little attempt, however, has been made to investigate the complex questions of heredity and biology. In place of the old explanation of a "social problem group", the inability of the multi-problem family to cope with its environment and to make use of the social services is now attributed to the "immature emotional development" of one or both of the spouses.

This approach owes much to social work and in particular to casework. Social workers in the health and welfare agencies have been faced with the consequences of inadequate social functioning, and at the same time they have become acutely aware of the failure of the social services to deal with individuals within the framework of the family group. Psychological and sociological studies of multi-problem families have been noticeably rare, and the majority of psychiatrists have had only slight contact with these families

In the United States over the past decade there have been important developments, from a fairly simple to a more sophisticated conceptual level. The outstanding leadership has come from the Community Research Associates and others associated with them. In 1952, the approach of family diagnosis having already been adopted in their work, criteria used in identifying multi-problem families focused on number and chronicity of problems in certain defined areas: chronic economic dependency, ill-health, and maladjustment. The presence of two of the three problems was considered sufficient to characterize the family as multi-problem. This method of identification still constitutes a main element in the definitions employed in studies in the United States and also in Canada.

In the St. Paul study (#172)[3], however, the concept of number and chronicity of problems has been replaced by a more sophisticated understanding. The focus shifted to the "level of functioning" of the family, which involved measurement of two criteria in a comprehensive system of classification: (a) the role performance of the members of the family, using nine categories of role performance, and (b) the level of social functioning in the family. The family was rated in terms of its adequacy on a seven-point scale.

With the San Mateo study (#130) a further shift in emphasis developed. The focus now turned to the problem area of maladjustment. Multi-problem families were characterized as pathological, and attention focused on the degree of pathology found in the family. Families were classified in terms of the level of their pathology, and treatment was determined according to this level.

A further refinement of this classification

in terms of the level of pathology included a diagnosis of pathological type. The works of Beisser (#110) and of Voiland (#281) describe and classify a range of family types, from the normal to the extreme pathological. Each type is characterized by a specific group of characteristics, and related to a level of pathology (Beisser).

The question arises as to the value of a concept which is so broad and comprehensive in character that it has come to include a heterogeneous collection of types of family and at times is used to indicate any family with problems so severe that it resists all efforts made towards its rehabilitation. For this reason several writers have urged that it is a useless concept and could profitably be abandoned.

At this point in the development of social work, however, there is merit in considering the positive aspects of the concept. Its main value appears to have been less as an incentive to greater sophistication in family diagnosis than as a spur to more critical thinking about the social services, their co-ordination, integration, and their planning. It has compelled us not only to examine the adequacy of the social services and of methods of professional social work in meeting the manifold and deep-seated needs of the family, but also to look beyond the present to the challenge of prevention. Both in Great Britain and in North America, although in different ways, the past decade has seen a variety of projects, studies, and fresh approaches to treatment in both statutory and voluntary agencies and in collaboration between the two.

II

Approaches to a Definition

The multi-problem family is much easier to describe than to define, and the majority of definitions found in the literature are in fact descriptions of its characteristics derived mainly from observation and experience in the field of social work. Research in the social sciences and in psychiatry has contributed comparatively little to definition. Our knowledge of causation still remains vague and imprecise.

In the preceding section reference was made to the lack of homogeneity in the concept. In Bowlby's words, "The problem family is not a unitary condition, it is a symptom with many different aetiologies."[4] Definitions tend to be of two broad categories: those which arise from the multi-problem family's failure to respond to society and to the social services; and those which emphasize the presence of specific problems in social functioning and in levels of pathology.

The former type of definition has been characteristic of the British approach to our subject; the latter, of the American. Hill (#186), for example, in discussing the generic features of families under stress, comments on this difference in approach: "Problem families became not so much victims of a poor distributive order as aggregates of neurotic or psychopathic individuals. More recently the work of Community Research Associates with problem families emphasizes the importance of the distortions of the marital axis, the incompatible combinations of personalities which make for divided and incompetent family headship." But it is easy to exaggerate this contrast. In quoting Siporin with approval[5] Hill overlooks the important developments in casework, during recent years in England, by the Family Service Units and by those departments of local authorities which have used the intensive casework approach.

Philp and Timms (#28) in their excellent survey also comment on differences between England and the United States in methods of helping the multi-problem family. But they point to another aspect: "In America where social work has developed rapidly on the technical side, the view has been expressed that 'the use of an "intensive" technique does not require different casework skills. It does require

a sharpening of the old skills.' In England the
special work of the Family Service Units and the
emphasis on practical help and material aid suggest
perhaps that new techniques have been found." But
in spite of differences in emphasis Philp and Timms
consider that in both England and America there is
general agreement that the basic technique is that
of support rather than the bringing about of personality change.

An English child psychiatrist (Ratcliffe, #14),
for example, states: "Problem families are those
which are constantly making demands on the social
agencies, which do not seem to make any progress
despite the help given to them, and which drift
from one agency to another." The Younghusband Committee in its report (#53, para. 316) wrote: "They
are only an entity in that they represent a problem
to society. The range of families grouped under
this heading is a wide one, and the results of inquiry do not go much beyond demonstrating the heavy
concentration of feeble-mindedness, emotional immaturity, inadequate personality development and lack
of sense of obligation in such families, compared
with the general run of the population." This committee, moreover, went on to observe that although
public attention is directed to dirt, squalor, malnutrition, delinquency, failure to pay the rent,
and to the unswept and ungarnished house, such a
house may sometimes provide a home and the "vitamins
of mental health". On the other hand, public attention has not been directed to the house which is
all too well swept and garnished but where the
children may suffer from emotional malnutrition
and neglect.

But, in spite of differences in approach and
of the limitations of definition, there is general
agreement over the main social characteristics of
the multi-problem family. Dirt, squalor, disease,
poverty and dependency, delinquency and crime, alcoholism, prostitution, child neglect, truancy,
mental deficiency, quarrelling between husband and
wife, and desertion have all been mentioned in numerous studies. The well-known problem classification developed by Community Research Associates

includes five categories:

1. Failure in the functioning of the mother.
2. Failure in the functioning of the father.
3. Failure in the functioning of the siblings.
4. Failure in marital adjustment.
5. Economic deprivation and grossly inadequate housing.

The New York City Youth Board (#220) in a study of 150 multi-problem families, using this method of classification, observed that 87 per cent had failures in three or more of these categories and 35 per cent in all five categories.

The State Charities Aid Association of New York, after an examination of many reports, put forward the following classification of characteristics (#221):

1. Multiplicity of problems.
2. Chronicity of need.
3. Resistance to treatment.
4. Handicapping attitudes, such as alienation from the community, hostility and suspicion towards authority.

In reporting on a survey undertaken by the Health Department of the London County Council, with the help of the Education and Welfare Departments, Dr. Scott (#33), the Medical Officer of Health, distinguished between potential problem families and hard-core problem families, basing the distinction on the difference in the number of points gained by the families when assessed according to characteristics such as the following: (in parents) low intelligence, mental illness, excessive drinking or gambling, criminal behaviour, cruelty to children, persistent quarrelling; (in children) repeated hospitalization, persistent truancy, delinquency, attendance at a child guidance clinic; (in housing) overcrowding, living in intolerable conditions; (in poverty and mismanagement) chronic debt, filth and disorder, lack of adequate furniture or clothing; (in general) failure to make use of help and service offered, children taken into care. The survey was based on the 400,000 families in the County of London with one or more children under 16 years of age. It showed a total of 2,239 potential and 783 hard-core problem families, a percentage of 0.75 of families at risk. The survey emphasized that in these families there is a high amount of emotional instability, of low intelligence, of known or suspected cruelty, of bad housing, and of rejection of help offered by the social services.

In a case study in Belgium based on families which had forfeited their parental rights, Debuyst, Renard, and Racine (#296) drew attention to the fact that the problem family corresponds in our society to a kind of socio-cultural under-development and stressed the following characteristics: low material standards of living in respect of housing, feeding, property, and rules of cleanliness; a high proportion of illiterate children; very large size of family; a low level of aspiration, absence of a sense of ambition, and a fatalistic attitude to life. The basic cause of these characteristics they attributed to a serious state of intellectual and emotional immaturity.

The relationship between multi-problem family behaviour and lower-class values is discussed later. At this point some emphasis should be placed on certain important characteristics which do not always emerge from studies focused on the problem, but some of which raise difficult and controversial issues in social policy:

1. The large size of the multi-problem family, which stands out in marked contrast to the general decrease in family size in Western industrialized society.
2. The high rate of mobility. Studies show that multi-problem families are frequently moving from one house to another, and often from one locality to another. This characteristic should also be related to the frequent

observations on their social isolation.
3. The multi-problem family is characterized by isolation and alienation from kinship group and neighbours. The popular image of a sub-cultural group of multi-problem families closely related to each other and collectively at variance with middle-class society is not supported by the literature.
4. A pattern of spouse relationships which one may describe as "matriarchal" or "role reversal". The former pattern seems to be most prevalent among lower-class Negroes in the United States and is characteristic of family structure in any social class where the partner is a transitory or absent member of the household. Role reversal takes place where there are emotionally dependent, alcoholic, or chronically ill fathers and where the mother is the more adequate partner.

To sum up this approach to definition, the term multi-problem family denotes those families which are of public concern because of their social and economic cost to the community and are characterized by:

1. A "pathological" family type as shown by (a) inadequate or destructive parent-child relationships by both parents, (b) inadequate social functioning on the part of parents and/or children, and (c) extreme emotional immaturity of either or both parents.
2. Dependent and/or exploitative behaviour towards the community and community agencies.
3. Persistent failure to respond to help or treatment offered.
4. A state of chronic dependency on the social services.

III

Social Functioning and Personality

Although the study of social characteristics may be useful for the purpose of detection, for the purpose of carrying out treatment, rehabilitation, and prevention, the help of the social sciences, psychiatry, and social work is required.

Approach to the problem, through the social functioning of the family, is still a relatively new method of study and treatment. It belongs particularly to the field of social work and draws on sociological theory for its basic concept of role. The family is seen as an open system of interdependent roles and relationships in which stress in the role performance of one member has consequences for related roles both inside and outside the family group. The use of role as a basic concept in family study carries with it two main advantages which are well illustrated in work with multi-problem families. In the first place, role provides a means of linking together the various areas of family functioning with the individual personalities of the members. Second, it provides a convenient research tool for evaluating family behaviour and for the assessment of change.

The family is analyzed in terms of its adequacy in the various areas of its functioning and in terms of the consequences of malfunctioning. A healthy family could be described as one where the instrumental functions (e.g., providing food, clothing, shelter) and its expressive functions (e.g., meeting the emotional needs of the children) are adequately fulfilled and where the family's relationship to the outside community is at best productive and co-operative, or at least "neutral". However, when the instrumental and expressive functions of the parents break down, and when relationships to the community give rise to conflict, exploitation, and chronic dependency, we consider the family to be "pathological". Its behaviour, as a whole, has destructive consequences to its own members and to society. Its pathology grows from the way in which the family malfunctions, that is, from its way of coping or problem-solving, from the way in which the members interact, and particularly from the way in which the parents rear their children. The pathological family type takes on its character from the personality types of its members, particularly from one or both parents.

Such an approach to the multi-problem family clearly requires a well-organized classification of pathological types of family in which the various kinds of malfunctioning are related to different types of personality in the family, but especially in the spouses. The work of the Community Research Associates is an outstanding indication of the development of such a classification, but there are still serious gaps in our knowledge. Existing attempts at classification, moreover, are related to the diagnostic stage, and the literature on treatment is focused mainly on broad general patterns of multi-problem family behaviour. A major obstacle in any such process arises from the conflicting demands of treatment and research. Treatment is based on assumptions about the dynamics of family relationships and on an approach to the family as a functioning or malfunctioning unit. Research, on the other hand, is concerned with the isolation of variables and with the measurement of their changing relationship with each other over time.

Geismar (#165) and Geismar and Ayres (#172) have described the St. Paul research approach to social functioning using a nine-category pattern, each with two to four sub-categories. This pattern comprises four areas within the family -- family relationships, child care and training, health practices, and household practices -- and three areas outside the family -- economic practices, social activities, and the use of community resources. The eighth area concerns relationships to the family-centred worker, and the ninth, individual behaviour and adjustment, that is, the way each family member performs his social role. Using community concern as a basis, they developed a seven-point scale of levels of functioning, ranging from "inadequate" through "marginal" to "adequate".

Two subsequent developments growing out of the work of the Community Research Associates under the direction of Bradley Buell, by Beisser (#110) and by Voiland (#281), are of importance in showing the relationship between differences in family type and levels of functioning and in going beyond those types of family generally labelled as multi-problem. The failure to analyze the social class membership of the families in their study makes it difficult to relate their work specifically to the multi-problem family. Only two of Beisser's five types and one of Voiland's four types appear to have relevance for the multi-problem family. On the other hand, both works throw light on the nature and multiplicity of problems, particularly in child rearing, among families outside the lower-class, and thus may perhaps contribute to the prevention of future multi-problem families.

These two typologies in outline are:

	Beisser	Voiland
Type 1	Normal	--
Type 2	Anxiety-ridden, perfectionistic	Perfectionistic
Type 3	Socially ineffective and unstable, parentally inadequate	Inadequate
Type 4	Socially adequate, parentally irresponsible	Egocentric
Type 5	Nonconforming, hostile	Unsocial

In the course of the San Mateo project, Buell, Beisser, and Wedemeyer (#130) were able to relate the five family types to three areas of family malfunctioning -- child rearing, marital, and economic. Although failure in child rearing was seen to be a common symptom of all family pathology, it expressed itself in particular and distinctive ways in each type.

Voiland's study in family casework diagnosis (#281) was based on an initial sample of 888 cases in contact with seven family casework agencies. An early attempt at classification of kind and degree of pathology in terms of the marital relationship provided no significant relationship. In the process of reformulation, a distinction was made between two kinds of family malfunctioning -- Level A and Level B, the former representing behaviour prohibited by specific laws or agency regulations having the force of law, the latter consisting of failures in social role responsibilities specified by some community health or welfare agency in contact with the family.

These two kinds of psychosocial disorder were then related to her four types of family.

During the testing of this classification on a total of 672 families in the public welfare demonstration projects in San Mateo, Winona, and Washington counties, 75 per cent of all the families served by public and private welfare agencies were found to have one or more of the principal Level A disorders. Her fourth and most pathological family type -- the unsocial -- is distinguished not only by a multiplicity of Level A disorders of a serious nature but by the presence of several serious Level B disorders as well. This "unsocial" type appears to be similar in some important respects to the multi-problem family.

Its main characteristics may be summarized as follows:

Family Type: Unsocial	This label denotes the family's lack of rapport with other people and with its environment. One or more of the following characteristics present: (a) paucity of ideals in the resolution of ordinary problems; (b) deviant social behaviour; (c) distorted thought processes and powers of concentration.

Psychosocial Disorders

Family:	More than one family member is personally and socially maladjusted to an extent that entails serious consequences, either social or legal. These handicaps adversely affect marital relationships, parent-child relationships, work habits, child development, and relationships within the community.
Adult:	Strong inclinations in the adult toward acting-out behaviour, delinquent conduct, and/or regression into psychosis. The presence of one or more of these responses in both partners distinguishes the unsocial family from other family types.
Children:	Level A disorders very likely to be present. The most frequent of these are delinquency, truancy, psychosis or severe personality disorders. The outstanding characteristic of Level B child disorders in the older child is his tendency to identify with one parent and to hold the other in low regard.

Classification of multi-problem families by family type carries with it the obvious weakness that it fails to distinguish between individual personality differences. A systematic analysis of individual personality is also required. The most commonly used diagnostic labels are "immature personality" and "character disorder" (of which the former term predominates in Great Britain and the latter in the United States and in Canada). Yet literature on personality in the field of dynamic personality is seriously lacking. The valuable study of character disorders in parents of delinquents (Reiner and Kaufman, #242) is one of the most useful works on character disorder.

The two main personality types emerging from a survey of the literature may be described as "emotionally immature". But they differ as to the ways in which this immaturity is shown, the ways which are used to cope with latent and overt problems, and the ways in which the families relate to external society and to the social services.

The personality type discussed in many papers (e.g., Fantl, #156; Henry, #185; Irvine, #16; Ratcliffe, #14) which appears to be most prevalent is the "passive dependent personality". As this label implies, these individuals when confronted with crisis, turn to sources outside the family. Their relationship to kinship groups, neighbours, the social services, and society in general appears to be one of a passive dependent kind, sometimes described as childish or immature. They are described by social workers as "incompetent", as having unrealistic levels of expectation, often arising from a non-recognition of reality, and as having an urgent need for immediate gratification of needs and goals. In Freudian terms they have been described as being "oral dependent" or as having a "weak ego". Some writers have also applied the label "ineducable", although new techniques of working with such individuals might negate the pessimism of this description.

In the British literature the passive dependent personality has been differentiated into two categories: (a) the emotionally retarded (i.e., those fixated at an early stage of emotional development); and (b) the emotionally regressed (those who have developed to a more mature level but have regressed because of environmental stress).

The passive dependent personality shows few signs of anxiety or neurosis and is generally classified under the heading of "character disorder". There is present, in addition, a very high incidence of chronic physical illness, possibly of psychogenic origin.

In contrast to this passive dependent personality is the other prevalent personality type, the "anti-social" personality (e.g., Bemmels, #111). The contrast is most acutely seen in the latter's exploitative attitudes and relationships with external society and with the social services. These individuals demand immediate gratification through aggressive behaviour and through the exploitation of the available resources. Their behaviour, although a sign of internal competence, implies a lack of concern and identification with others, an egocentricity and narcissism, and an inadequate super-ego. For this reason they have been classified by some writers as psychopathic or sociopathic personalities exhibiting asocial types of behaviour. Some workers and doctors have labelled them as "ineducable" in so far as traditional techniques of working with them have proved inadequate in bringing about change.

They share with the passive dependent personality a lack of anxiety and guilt. Moreover, among both types there is evidence of adult crime, juvenile delinquency, and near-delinquent behaviour. But this delinquency varies in kind. Some is based on the tendency of the anti-social personality to "act out", a characteristic not found in the "passive dependent personality". So far as juvenile delinquency is concerned, a recent study (Wilson, #49) emphasizes the prevalence of "neglect delinquency" as contrasted with other kinds. At "Seaport", Wilson observed that juvenile delinquency in problem families was eight times as high as the general rate for the city.

The following is an attempt at classification in terms of the two main types of personality:

Emotionally immature	
Type I Passive dependent	Type II Anti-social and asocial

Way of coping
  passive dependency on external sources
	Way of coping
	  aggressive and exploitative behaviour to external persons and groups

Characteristics
  generally incompetent
  "ineducable"
  immediate gratification of needs and goals
  passive
	Characteristics
	  competent
	  "ineducable"
	  immediate gratification of needs and goals
	  acting-out
	  narcissistic, egocentric
	  lack of concern, identification and respect for others

weak ego control "oral dependent" unrealistic level of expectation and non-recognition of reality	inadequate super-ego
lack of anxiety and guilt chronic illness	lack of anxiety and guilt
some juvenile delinquency	prevalence of crime and juvenile delinquency

In all personality types in multi-problem families may be found various forms of mental illness and emotional disturbance. One overt manifestation of these is in the various forms of addiction. The addiction most frequently referred to is that of alcoholism, but reference is also made to compulsive gambling and spending.

Precise knowledge as to the relationship between dimensions of personality and types of treatment is greatly needed, though in the case of so amorphous a category as the multi-problem family it will not be readily acquired. A study by a psychologist[6] into the classification of delinquents with implications for treatment is, however, of relevance. Argyle distinguishes, from a review of the psychological literature, between four relatively independent types of delinquents, and examines research findings as to appropriate treatment: (1) inadequate super-ego; (2) deviant identifications; (3) weak ego control; and (4) lack of sympathy.

For the first type the need is for intensive contact with at least one person in authority, with whom a close relationship is established and on whom the client becomes dependent for approval. Firm demands must be made and approval withdrawn if these are not complied with. For the second type the treatment indicated is separation of the delinquent from the peer group and re-establishment in a primarily non-delinquent environment, where he may identify with non-delinquent models. The third type requires a firm supportive environment, probably involving continuous relationships with other people, leading to a strengthening of ego control. The fourth type may benefit from satisfactory experiences with the peer group, as can be secured through group therapy, a form of treatment which, it may be noted, was contra-indicated in the case of those with deviant identifications.

The variety of forms of ancillary treatment which may be combined with the fundamental casework relationship makes it necessary for us to improve our classification of personality types so as to make provision, whenever possible, for appropriate forms of treatment.

The question of the intelligence of the multi-problem family is still open to argument, but there is good reason to believe that many of the earlier studies which emphasized intellectual defect in multi-problem family aetiology, using the label "ineducable" (Blacker, #7, Sheridan, #34) failed to take adequate account of the consequences of emotional retardation. Thus, systematic study of intelligence is an important gap in the literature.

IV

Social Class and Environment

The association between families with low standards of living and slums is supported by a long tradition of social observation and reform. Poor families and poor housing have generally been found in the same areas, not only in large cities but also in the village and in the small town. Booth's study of Life and Labour of the People in London[7] was one of the first surveys to emphasize the close connection between poverty and overcrowding. In the United States the ecological school of sociology at Chicago, pioneered by Professors Burgess and Park, gave rise to new knowledge about the distribution of social problems in relation to the "natural" areas of a city. Shaw and McKay[8] pointed out, through the use of radial and zone maps, that rates of crime and delinquency were highest in the centre of the city, and that these "delinquency areas" were neighbourhoods of physical deterioration, of declining population (due to commercial and industrial invasion), of high economic dependency, of high concentration of Negro and a succession of foreign-born groups, of proximity to areas of industrial concentration, and of social disintegration. Faris and Dunham[9] observed, in their study of mental illness, that schizophrenia was concentrated in old central slum districts of Chicago. This concentration they explained in terms of the social disorganization of these areas and the isolation of the people living in them. Later writers, however, have preferred the explanation of conflicting norms to "disorganization" and have pointed to the fact that the norms of these areas are often highly organized.

The ecological approach when later applied to Great Britain, especially in delinquency studies, showed certain important differences from the American studies. Whereas in the American studies crime and delinquency decrease in size the farther one moves from the interstitial areas near the centre of the city, in Great Britan the nature of the physical environment (Morris[10]) appears to bear little relation to the location of delinquency areas. Several studies (Mannheim[11], Spencer[12], Jones[13]) emphasized the high rate of delinquency in new municipal housing areas, many of them on the periphery of the city. It is significant that many of these areas contained a high proportion of families previously living in slums and poor central areas.

Although ecological studies of multi-problem families have been less numerous and extensive than those of crime and delinquency, the available evidence points to a similar pattern of distribution and to attempts at explanation along similar lines. Both types of behaviour appear to be particularly characteristic of lower-class families living in poor areas, though not exclusively in deteriorated housing.

More important than purely ecological explanations, however, is the concept of anomie (absence of rules to live by). Merton's[14] development of this concept has given rise to several important studies in the field of deviant behaviour. The basic assumption of Merton's theory is dissociation between the goals of society and the means of achieving those goals. Merton postulates four types of deviant or non-conformist behaviour. Of these types, two seem especially relevant for the multi-problem family, "innovation" and "retreatism". The former type is characteristic of individuals who accept the goals of their society but reject the conventional methods of achieving them. Crime and delinquency are typical non-conformist methods of achieving these goals. The criminal strives after material possessions through the use of illegitimate means. The latter type of behaviour, "retreatism", differs from "innovation" in that it rejects both the goals and the means of achieving them. The retreatist, in fact, unlike the innovator, gives up the struggle for achievement and success through conventional methods and drifts along in a private world, isolated and alienated from ordinary society.

Two other studies, by Cohen[15] and by Cloward and Ohlin[16], have made valuable developments in Merton's theory. Although their primary focus has been delinquent behaviour by juvenile groups, their theory may also be applied to the multi-problem family. Cohen's primary concern is the reaction of young people who are denied the means of access to middle-class goals and the delinquency which follows as a consequence of this denial. Cloward and Ohlin put forward hypotheses designed to explain the variety of methods adopted by adolescent groups who are unable to use legitimate methods of achieving the goals of society and for whom illegitimate methods are more readily available.

It is important to see these studies within the framework of social class. In spite of the growing literature on class, it is difficult to locate the multi-problem family clearly within the class structure, and this is obviously an area in need of further research. A major reason for this difficulty arises from differences in the ways in which the middle class and the lower class look at social differences. (To use "working class in place of "lower class" would fail to take account of the distinctive characteristics of lower-class society.) Dahrendorf[17] distinguishes between two ways of looking at class, the "hierarchical" and the "dichotomous". Those "above" in the class structure see society as a continuous hierarchy of positions, while those "below" are struck by the gap between themselves and the "others". "Subjected groups," in Dahrendorf's words, "tend to emphasize the cleavages that in their opinion account for the deprivations which they feel."

Thus, in attempting to relate the multi-problem family to the class structure, this distinction in ways of looking at class usefully points up the feeling of isolation and alienation found in case studies. It may be particularly relevant in the case of Merton's response of innovation. This same distinction may also be helpful in explaining the frequently observed gap in communication between the social services and the multi-problem family.

The relevance of all these studies is closely linked with the concept of a lower-class subculture. Multi-problem families in certain respects identify themselves with the norms and aspirations of the lower class. Lower-class culture can be seen both negatively and positively; both are relevant to the understanding of the multi-problem family. From the negative point of view it is seen as a denial of the middle-class way of life. The workers who come into contact with these families are usually middle-class in their values. They see the multi-problem family as resistant to middle-class standards of housekeeping, child rearing, and social morality. Seen positively, conformity to lower-class culture involves conformity to its values, its language, dress, the community of the street and informal group, the attitudes to higher-class groups, the unstable structure of the family based on inadequate fathers or on frequently-absent fathers on the periphery of the family leading to a process of role reversal in the spouses (#22) or to the mother-dominated household.

Side by side with strong feelings of community go suspicion of outsiders, exploitation of the social services, distrust of middle-class standards in relation to such behaviour as gambling or stealing. To describe lower-class culture, however, as "disorganized" is to use middle-class patterns of formal associations as a criterion of organization and to neglect the equally important informal associations of street corner, door step, or "pubs".

The understanding of lower-class culture is of particular importance for two reasons: first, for its effect on the family and the socialization of the child; and second, for its denial of middle-class aspirations and expectations of upward mobility. Many studies have commented (e.g., Spinley[18], Wilson, #49) on the inadequacy of the child-rearing patterns in slum and multi-problem families -- their failure to give any clear standards of behaviour or to put before the children any clear image of the role of father, husband, mother, wife, which they can incorporate into their own character development and use as a model for later adult behaviour. Hence the continuation of similar role behaviour that takes place from one generation to another.

Miller (#211) writes: "The nature of social groupings in the lower-class community may be clarified if we make the assumption that it is the one-sex peer unit rather than the two-parent family unit which represents the most significant relational unit for both sexes in lower-class communities." Thus the lower-class family has a social and psychological function for the individual very different from that of the middle-class family. In describing it, moreover, it is deceptively easy to use labels which, whether moral or non-moral, such as "living in sin" or "broken home", make use of middle-class terminology without recognizing the different significance this behaviour has for the lower class.

Understanding of lower-class family behaviour has been greatly clarified by social investigations of lower-class culture in under-developed areas, such as Jamaica (Braithwaite[19], Rodman[20]) in which illegitimacy arising from the mother-dominated lower-class household is not stigmatized as a deviation from middle-class standards but is regarded as a natural concomitant of the social and economic structure of the society. Kerr[21] has pointed out the similarity in Rorschach test results between families in a Liverpool slum and lower-class Jamaicans. Similar observations have been applied to lower-class Negro culture in the United States.

Characteristic of this type of culture is the absence of child-rearing patterns directed towards self-improvement and upward mobility. The pattern of delinquency associated with these families has been labelled by one recent writer (Wilson, #49) as "neglect delinquency", a way of behaving not necessarily inculcated by their elders but a method, learned in infancy, of getting the ordinary satisfactions and possessions of which they are denied. Some studies (Miller, #211, #Kasius, 195) have observed the "fatalism" of lower-class culture, its reliance on chance, luck, fate, as shown, for example, by the popularity of various forms of gambling, and its belief in forces outside the control of the individual. Success is just a matter of the "luck of the draw" rather than the result of the middle-class virtues of effort and hard work.

But there is also evidence to suggest that multi-problem families cannot be seen exclusively as members of lower-class society. First, we must question whether it is sensible to treat these families as persons clearly identified with any defined group of standards and values. In some multi-problem families, for example, one or both of the spouses may be downwardly mobile and have drifted into this group through lack of intelligence, character disorder, or social circumstance. They may still cherish a hope that their children will retrieve their parents' loss in status. Second, we must distinguish between real and nominal values. Baldamus and Timms (#4), in examining the relevance of Merton's concept of retreatism as an explanation of problem family behaviour, conclude that "the conventional concept of standards (or norms) of conduct should be broken up into 'nominal' and 'real' standards." Whereas deviant behaviour in matters such as child care or cleanliness may occur in multi-problem families at the same time as there is superficial or nominal agreement with approved standards, in other matters (e.g., the image of the ideal neighbour) their behaviour is consistent with a clearly defined sub-culture. Baldamus and Timms put forward the following hypothesis: the more extreme cases of retreatism are characterized by weak or poorly articulated goals together with real (deviant) standards, while at the other end of the scale there is a combination of strong and nominal conformity to generally accepted standards.

While the validity of their hypothesis still remains to be tested, the good sense of this important distinction between "real" and "nominal" standards is obvious. Multi-problem families, like other families, are affected by the standards expressed by the mass media of press, television, and radio, and they are also aware of the expectations of behaviour held by those who represent the health and welfare services, such as welfare workers and public health nurses. They may give overt allegiance to certain standards without at the same time possessing the ability to understand or to achieve them. In a study of multi-problem families in London (Ontario), Veitch (#59) concluded that there was little evidence to support the hypothesis that the multi-problem family forms a separate sub-culture. "Many of their values are essentially middle-class values. That they hold these values, but fail to achieve middle-class standards, has been apparent. However, in this study we see that they largely identify with middle-class standards which they see as desirable, but which they have been frustrated in achieving."

The third reason is closely related to this

point -- the weakness of the concept of sub-culture as an explanation of the deviance of the multi-problem family. It is certainly attractive to view these families as subscribing to a set of standards and values at variance with the dominant middle-class culture. Indeed, there is some evidence to suggest that they are happy to remain encapsulated within the sub-culture of a group of similar families in street or block of streets. But as a general explanation the concept is unsatisfactory because it fails to take account of the serious state of isolation in which these families appear to live. They are isolated not merely from their kinship group but also from friends and neighbours, and thus unable to draw on an important source of mutual aid and help in time of need and crisis. In this respect the multi-problem family stands in marked contrast to traditional working-class society both in the United States and in Great Britain (Young and Willmott[22], Bott[23], Rainwater[24]). The multi-problem family, as Wilson concludes (#49), should be seen "not as a manifestation of a specific sub-culture, but as an index of the breakdown of a culture."

The residential mobility of the multi-problem family, a fact observed in many studies, is also evidence of its isolation from neighbourhood ties. Lacking roots in a local community the family moves from place to place. But, unlike the middle-class family, it lacks the ability to use the social services in a constructive way. Moreover, it frequently threatens those who live in the immediate locality, especially those who are aspiring in their standards. As Booth recognized, "those most injured by the depressed poverty of others, were those who are themselves only a little removed from the same condition; whose life is dragged down by their unfortunate, or weak, or worthless neighbours . . ."[25]

It seems fair to conclude that the consequences of lower-class culture are seen to be most serious in the defective rearing and socialization of children on the part of the multi-problem family. Physical environment is certainly of far less consequence than family structure and the standards associated with it. But this structure is itself part of the economic and social framework of the lower class, and it is for this reason that any rehabilitative policy faces formidable obstacles to change.

V

Treatment

The trend in treatment and methods of rehabilitation is clear and unmistakable. It is the recognition of the failure of an approach by individual services to individual members of the multi-problem family, particularly in times of crisis. Again and again in numerous studies we find evidence of overlapping of services, each with a concern for a different problem and frequently for a different member of the family (e.g., #46, #55, #129). Dirt, sickness, delinquency, child neglect, poverty, unemployment, excessive drinking, sexual promiscuity, and other problems have at different times given rise to attempts at treatment from workers in the services concerned. But their contacts have usually been short-lived, continuing only while the crisis lasts.

Thus there have been three main obstacles to effective help apart from the outstanding question of diagnosis, which is discussed in Section III. These are the fragmentation and lack of coordination among the health and welfare services, the fact that each of these services has tended to focus on a particular symptom, generally of an individual family member, and the absence of continued long-term contact between client and worker beyond dealing with the need at the particular moment of crisis.

It is in the light of these three obstacles

that methods of treatment, whether directed to
individuals or to families or to communities,
have developed during the post-war years. We
cannot do better than adopt the useful classification devised by Lagey and Ayres in their report
of a survey of multi-problem family projects in
all communities of 100,000 or over in North
America:

1. The case conference approach.
2. The intensive casework approach.
3. The multi-service approach using
   a planned combination of casework,
   group work, community organization,
   and health and rehabilitation services.
4. The community development approach.
5. Other less common approaches such as
   volunteer case aides, homemaker
   services, and residential training programs.

To this last category we should perhaps add the
special housing projects directed mainly to
multi-problem families.

The publication of this comprehensive survey
by Lagey and Ayres makes it redundant to include
here more than comment on certain features of
these developments, particularly in view of
British experience, which is not included in
their survey. The first point is covered in
their justification for the survey itself. It is
abundantly clear that concern over the multi-
problem family has stimulated a proliferation of
projects all over North America, many of which
are neither grounded on prior experience elsewhere
nor co-ordinated with one another so that there
may be opportunities for the comparison of
achievement. The organization of these projects,
moreover, tends to exclude the use of methods for
their evaluation.

Second, is the popularity of the intensive
casework approach. Of the 117 projects from 76
communities which they analyzed, 38 per cent fell

into this category. This confirms our general assumption that the main impetus to change has been the recognition on the part of caseworkers that intensive family-centred work, using "aggressive" or "reaching out" techniques and focused on improvement in social functioning and relationships both within the family and with community agencies, offers the most promising opportunities for change. At the same time it is increasingly recognized that in addition to intensive casework there is a serious need for co-ordinated and integrated planning among the diversity of agencies, both public and private, which are involved in giving service to the multi-problem family.

Social Casework

The major role which casework has come to assume in the treatment of the multi-problem family is a comparatively recent development, and casework as a whole has undoubtedly benefited from it. Such phrases as "reaching out", "hard to reach", and "aggressive casework" are indicative of the changed response of caseworkers to the resistance shown by the multi-problem family towards offers of help.

Although a very great deal of work still remains to be done in classifying diagnostic types in the multi-problem family, certain basic principles in the casework approach are generally agreed upon. These arise from a number of factors. Foremost are the barriers of mutual hostility and suspicion between the family and the community. The social services, both public and private, are seen by the family as part of a system of values which is alien to their own, and as providing material resources to be exploited rather than as offering help in effecting change in social functioning. Caseworkers have thus come to see the necessity of taking into account a basic difference in values between the middle-class world of the social agency and lower-class society with which the multi-problem family is often identified. Fantl (#156) emphasizes as examples of this contrast in values the areas of child-rearing practices, the expression of anxiety and aggression, multiplicity of standards in the use of language or other symbolic behaviour, and discrimination.

Second, are the consequences of personal inadequacy, persistent failure, hopelessness, and rejection. The multi-problem carries with it the scars of past struggles to solve some of the basic problems of family living, the search for employment, the furnishing of a home, the feeding and clothing of children. Life has been lived at a primitive level and persistent failure has led to a sense of resignation with this level and little effective motivation to achieve anything more. The family develops a pattern of dependency on outside sources for the fulfillment of its basic needs, particularly economic needs.

Third, the effects of immature and inadequately socialized personalities are seen both in the internal roles and relationships of the family members and in their relationships with the community outside. These deficiencies in socialization often seem to be transmitted from one generation to the next, and it is natural that "preventive intervention" should focus especially on the child-rearing functions. The consequences of immaturity and of character disorders show themselves in different ways -- in conflict with the law, marital quarrels, addiction to alcohol, reckless gambling and credit-buying, prostitution, and illegitimate children. Yet in spite of this, writers have also commented on the ties of affection that keep the family together. There are certain positive strengths in the multi-problem family on which caseworkers are able to build.

Casework literature now stresses the importance of the family-centred approach in both diagnosis and treatment. Seeing the members in the process of interaction with one another is particularly useful in the case of multi-problem families, since their ability to verbalize is usually very limited. The family provides the obvious setting, moreover, in which the skills in interpersonal relationships, which are so lacking in multi-problem families, can be learned and may then perhaps be carried over into relationships outside the family. In the St. Paul project (Geismar and Ayres, #169), family solidarity was found to be the most significant factor in growth. If such solidarity can be strengthened, the prospects for change are greater. Lack of identity and self-esteem are common problems, and if the family can be helped to agree on small goals, the individual members may derive ego support from the rest of the group and a sense of solidarity and identity may be gained through a joint effort.

The role of the caseworker with the multi-problem family has been usefully summarized by Wiltse (#292) as that of "parenting". Under this term he includes five functions: (1) to give consistent warmth of feeling and concern for each person -- in other words to love; (2) to offer oneself as an ego ideal; (3) to teach by precept and example; (4) to supervise and set limits; and (5) to join actively with the family in seeking improvement of the family's welfare, its social status, and opportunities for its members to exploit their talents towards the same end.

The method of "reaching out" involves the caseworker in a supportive and a teaching role as well as in an understanding use of authority. Frankness, directness, and honesty on the part of the worker were found to be important in the Syracuse (Weinandy, #285) and the St. Paul (Overton and Tinker, #233) studies. The caseworker has the responsibility of explaining the expectations of society and the limits to the degree of nonconformity which society may reasonably tolerate. Such a process takes place within a "partnership", as Overton[26] has described the relationship between family and caseworker in the St. Paul study.

It is abundantly clear from the literature that this form of casework demands professional skill and maturity of judgment of a very high order and a supportive agency framework within which to work. Diagnosis involves the complex process of assessing a wide variety of factors, both psychological and sociological. The "impulse-ridden client", to use Reiner and Kaufman's (#242) perceptive phrase, has deep unconcious needs which can be understood only by reference to his early stages of development. Radcliffe (#14) also has emphasized the inadequate gratification of early dependency needs which has led to arrested emotional development. At the same time, multi-problem families have nearly all suffered from serious economic stress, some for long periods and under such circumstances as would have defeated even the most mature and resourceful families without support from external sources such as kin and friends (Wilson, #49).

But in addition to the complexity of diagnosis and the working through of the barriers of resistance, apathy, and hopelessness, the caseworker also has a major task of interpretation and of co-ordination of the other services concerned with the family. In England the work of the Family Service Units is an example of this latter role. By assuming the major responsibility for problem families in certain areas, the F.S.U. worker comes to occupy an interpretative and co-ordinating role vis-a-vis other services which have statutory responsibilities to perform. In the United States, Bemmels (#111) stresses the value of this function in a study of seven fighting families sponsored by the Research Department of the New York City Youth Board. In the San Mateo study, Buell, Beisser, and Wedemeyer (#130) observed that success or failure in achieving integration of services rested in the last analysis with the caseworker to whom the case had been assigned. Professional caseworkers also have an important supervisory role in relation to the voluntary workers and case-aides whose services are useful in numerous ways, especially in the organization of children's activities.

Much work still remains to be done on the meaning and evaluation of change. Using the Geismar-Ayres approach to the measurement of family functioning (#172; see also Geismar, #165), the St. Paul study was able to report improved social functioning in two-thirds of the families. Change, however, is not uniform in all the areas. The Boston Chronic Problem Family study in a report on preliminary findings on 27 families (Stone, Zilbach, Hurwitz, and Idelson, #264) pointed to some contrasts in change occurring during treatment. For example, in socialization patterns (as shown by discipline) fathers changed proportionately more often than did mothers; in the parental roles fathers changed most as fathers and least as breadwinners, while the mothers, on the other hand, showed most improvement as housekeepers and least as community members, thus showing a reverse pattern of change in their primary social role.

To summarize, caseworkers have clearly shown the value of the "reaching out" approach to treatment. There is general agreement on the family-centred approach, on the need for very limited but clearly defined goals, and on the length of time taken before the family's protective screen of tightness and resistance begins to give way to more neurotic symptoms, thus making possible the growth of a deeper relationship with the caseworker.

Co-ordination of Services

The literature provides abundant illustrations of the variety of social services, both public and private, to which the multi-problem family is known. This, in itself, is not surprising. It is axiomatic, in view of the definition of multiplicity of problems, that a multiplicity of services should be involved with them. What has given rise to greater concern, however, is the unplanned and unsystematic basis on which these services are provided. The chronicity of its problems emphasizes the length of time during which a family is in contact with the services, and some studies have drawn attention to the extent to which this contact is maintained from one generation to the next.

Criticism has been directed particularly at two issues. The first is the sporadic nature of the contacts, and the second is the multiplicity of services concerned and the likelihood of duplication of work. The multi-problem family tends to seek help primarily at time of crisis and to discontinue contact with the services until a further crisis occurs. The family's expectation of the nature of the service has been, at least in the past, for material help in cash or in kind. The idea of treatment in the sense of casework or psychiatric help or community or recreational services has appeared strange. But provision of service largely on a basis of what may be called crisis-orientation carries with it serious weaknesses. It provides no opportunity for long-term and continuing work. It is in the context of this system of sporadic contact that the multi-problem family's "intractability" must be seen. The pattern is familiar, in which short-run progress is not maintained during absence of contact with the service.

The second issue has been constantly noted in both the European and American literature, and has been observed in studies of individual cases as well as in quantitative analyses. The conclusions of the Community Research Associates have been continually quoted. In St. Paul, some 90 public and private services were helping 23 per cent of the community's 100,000 families in which one or more of the three problems had resulted in disorganized family life. It was a small proportion of families (6 per cent) that consumed well over half of the professional skill of these 90 agencies. In the four communities studied, this small group of families occupied between 70 and 88 per cent of the total relief load, from 65 to 90 per cent of the total health service load, and from 43 to 56 per cent of the load carried by mental health, casework, and correctional services. However, in a recent Toronto study (#77) of a sample of 1,690 families and individuals served by health and welfare services, less than 10 per cent of the sample were receiving service from three or more organizations.

Thus, the multi-problem family serves to focus attention on a question of major importance in the administration of the social services, their planning, integration, and co-ordination. Services tend to have grown up piecemeal and not in response to a well co-ordinated plan. They have been designed predominantly for the individual rather than the family, and each service tends to have responsibility for one particular symptom of disorganization. Many of the responsibilities assumed by the public services have been laid down by statute, and informal arrangements to vary them meet with difficulties.

It is certainly attractive to seek a remedy for a state of affairs which is clearly undesirable in its consequences for the family in a fundamental reorganization of services -- by the creation of a single family and child agency, for example, or by the creation of a new municipal department responsible for preventive functions, at present distributed over several departments. The latter proposal was strongly recommended by some witnesses to the Ingleby Committee[27] in the course of its inquiry into the prevention of child neglect in England and Wales. But the implications of a fundamental reorganization of services extend far beyond the welfare of the multi-problem family and are closely related to the political and administrative framework of the country involved.

Here we can do no more than indicate certain basic principles and general trends of development.

In Great Britain both the Younghusband Committee (#53) and the Ingleby Committee in their reports emphasized the importance of effective machinery for the co-ordination of services and of flexibility in departmental boundaries within local authorities (municipalities). The Younghusband Committee examined in considerable detail the operation of the statutory local authority co-ordinating committees which had been set up in 93 per cent of all authorities since the Government circulars of 1950. Three points on this method in their report are of particular interest. First, the need for systematic research into the use of this method; second, the need to distinguish between the functions of a co-ordinating committee in working out general questions of principle and policy and those of a case conference of the workers involved in a family in planning treatment; and third, the statement that, although current views on multiplicity of visits were often overstated, good team-work required an administrative structure which would facilitate co-operation and opportunities for regular meetings and discussions at all levels. The Ingleby Committee did not propose the setting up of any new department, such as a local authority family and child service, nor of uniform machinery for co-ordination of local services, but did recommend that there should be a statutory obligation on all local authorities to submit for Government approval schemes for the prevention of child neglect.

In the United States and Canada many of the same difficulties over the co-ordination of services arise. Many projects have been set up with the object of improved co-ordination and of reducing the number of services involved in helping the multi-problem family. The work of the referral units of the New York City Youth Board (#181) is an excellent example. But, although the obstacles to uniformity among municipalities are much greater in federal countries with three levels of government, the departments of Public Welfare have under their jurisdiction a wider range of services than in Great Britain and consequently a greater opportunity for taking a leading role in co-ordinating services for the multi-problem family. This role is discussed further under the heading "Prevention". For several reasons the conclusion seems unavoidable that the present proliferation of multi-problem family projects surveyed by Lagey and Ayres must give way in the course of time to the growth of systematic plans for case classification in public welfare departments and for the location of the major responsibility for co-ordination with caseworkers in them.

Prevention

Closely related to the problem of the co-ordination of services is the formidable task of discovering effective ways of preventing the occurrence of the multiplicity of problems characteristic of the multi-problem families. The very chronicity and persistence of crises in these families, and of their failure in social functioning, show why prevention is among the most difficult problems in the whole field of social work and social welfare.

The concept of prevention is used in such different senses that it is frequently misleading in its implications. Until about 1955 its use in social work in the United States was largely avoided, and when introduced in the public health sense it was often used in a "distorted and confusing manner" (Rapaport[28]). Of the three categories of prevention -- primary, secondary, and teriary -- the secondary, or preventive intervention, i.e., the detection of a problem at a point of mild disturbance and the prevention of chronicity, is the most hopeful approach. It is, moreover, closely related to treatment.

Prevention in the primary sense is a long-term operation, and, as Buell (#128) recognized, the reduction of multiple causes is a possibility only in the course of two or three generations.[29] Several studies have shown the relationship between successive generations of multi-problem families (e.g., #55, #58). But the process of intervening in what appears to be a vicious circle requires greater knowledge of aetiology than we possess at the present time, and it involves also a wide range of services concerned with health and welfare. Above all, perhaps, it requires a continued and systematic reduction of Beveridge's giant evils of Want, Disease, Ignorance, Squalor, and Idleness.[30]

Prevention of dependency in the primary sense

is closely related to the social and economic structure of a society, to the level of employment, to opportunities for social mobility, to discrimination against minority groups, and to social policy in the field of wages and social security. It is, in any case, difficult to discern the consequences of improvements in economic and social policy on multi-problem families, who constitute a residual group in our society.

Buell (#129) has summarized the range of community services and the basic elements in their framework which appear important in any future preventive program. His conclusion that "it is impossible to identify with assurance any agency which occupies an unquestioned pivotal relation to the community program for prevention and protection against the consequences of maladjustment" raises again the difficult question of co-ordination. Coherence in the planning of the health and welfare services is an essential element in any general plan of prevention.

Although social scientists have become increasingly skeptical of the usefulness of searching for the causes of social breakdown, even in the case of more homogeneous forms of behaviour, certain broad trends in the development of the health and welfare services deserve emphasis. In spite of important differences between Canada and the United States and Great Britain of size, levels of government, administration, and policy, there is a general movement towards a more systematic approach to earlier detection and classification of families in trouble. At the same time, the obstacles to effective prevention presented by the multiplicity of services, each concerned with a specific problem or family member, are now recognized.

In Britain both the Ingleby and the Younghusband Committees commented on the piecemeal development of the social services. In examining the problem of neglected children the Ingleby Committee distinguished three stages in the prevention of neglect: (a) the detection of families at risk; (b) the investigation and diagnosis of the particular problem; and (c) treatment -- the provision of facilities and services to meet the families' needs and to reduce the stresses and dangers that they face. The Committee felt that there was some confusion about these different stages and their relative importance. A wide variety of workers and agencies have opportunity for detecting the family at risk -- neighbours, doctors, teachers, health nurses, and social workers of different kinds. As one method of facilitating the referral cases to the department best suited to give skilled diagnosis, the Committee recommended the setting up in larger areas of a family advice centre as a central point of reference.

The Younghusband Committee (#53) pointed out the necessity not only of assessing a situation but also of identifying the greater or lesser degree of skill required of the social worker. The Committee identified three categories of need, ranging from straightforward or obvious needs requiring some simple service, to problems of special difficulty requiring skilled professional help. A high proportion of multi-problem families would be expected to fall in this third category, but the Committee emphasized the importance of a variety of studies to determine different types of need and the most appropriate ways of meeting them.

In the United States and Canada the same need for early detection of child neglect in its various forms and for the more systematic classification of family disorders has been observed. Departments of Public Welfare, on whom the burden of economic dependency largely rests, have a major responsibility in the development of better methods of classifying the various levels of family breakdown. Studies such as the Washington County (#153), the San Mateo (#130), the Winona County Work Reorientation Projects (#176)[31], and the Family Reorientation Program of Douglas County (#152) are illustrations of this trend.

The Family Reorientation Program of Douglas County introduced a systematic plan of classification for the total public assistance caseload according to the kind and amount of social service required. It defined three levels of social service: Level I, families presenting very complex mental and personality problems; Level II, families with multiple difficulties of a less serious nature; and Level III, families in which financial aid is the primary need. In January 1962 it was found that 17.6 per cent of all the families with children on the county's caseload should be receiving Level I service; 44.8 per cent, Level II; and 37.6 per cent, Level III.

In Canada the Public Welfare Division of the Canadian Welfare Council has drawn up a system of classification for a public assistance caseload and criteria for the allocation of cases to categories according to the kind of service required.

There is no clear line of demarcation between prevention and treatment. This trend in classification, therefore, deserves to be considered from both points of view. Although it seems obvious that the multi-problem family should be assigned to the more skilled and experienced of the professional social work staff for intensive treatment, there remains the difficult question of priorities. Decisions as to the amount of money and time to be devoted to the hard core of the total public welfare caseload can be taken only in the light of the general availability of public resources. The effectiveness of such decisions will depend, in part at least, on continued experiment and research with stratified samples of different types of case. Such experiments may have a preventive value in helping with the diagnosis and treatment of the potential multi-problem family.

Other Ancillary Services

The range of services which have some contribution to make towards improvement in the condition of multi-problem families is both wide and varied. Emphasis in this report has been placed on casework services, which have a major treatment and co-ordinating role, and on the difficult questions of co-ordination and treatment. The term "ancillary" is used to suggest that the multi-problem family has many needs, for which a variety of services is necessary at different stages in treatment and for different members of the family. Here we deal briefly with the main categories.

Neighbourhood and community services

The approach of the Settlement House in slum areas of large cities in the United States, Canada, and Britain carries with it a long tradition of philanthropy and service. It grew from the recognition of great pioneers that the social and recreational needs of families living in these areas were such that special help was needed in them. A higher level of living, the extension of social services, and slum clearance and neighbourhood improvement schemes have all contributed substantially to the reduction of poverty and distress and to healthier living. But the fact remains that multi-problem families are still most likely to be found in the poorest central areas, or if not there, in public housing or housing projects in newer residential districts.

Thus, certain neighbourhoods still remain an important focus of social action, and projects for community organization and community development carry with them potential benefits to multi-problem families as well as to other families living in the area. Such projects may have a variety of objects in mind, of which some have been performed in the past by Settlement Houses and others are associated with Neighbourhood and Family Centres (e.g., the Huntington Family Center--Junior League Project in Syracuse, #300). The development of recreational programs, parks and open spaces, the encouragement of citizens' committees and public action to prevent deterioration in housing conditions, and projects for delinquency prevention are examples of this function.

The multi-problem family now emerges as a focus of neighbourhood concern, and useful experiments on a neighbourhood basis are either in operation or at the planning stage. The Area Demonstration Project in Vancouver, British Columbia (#61), for example, aims at the creation of a neighbourhood house with the intention of providing the basic health, welfare, and recreation services to all residents in the area, with intensive services for multi-problem families. In particular, the family general practitioner is to be closely related with the family treatment plan and a systematic study made of genetic, biological, psychiatric, psychological, and social factors associated with the multi-problem families.

In a New Haven housing development a project (#217) is concerned with the provision of intensive casework from existing agencies together with special group work--recreation services in the housing area and the co-ordination of neighbourhood services. Several projects, in Canada and the United States (e.g., #60, #65, #66, #144) have been set up through neighbourhood houses providing limited service on a joint casework--group work basis. In New York the Interdepartmental Neighborhood Service Center in Central Harlem (#197) was established in 1959 as a pilot project of the Office of the Mayor with the object of providing a unified approach to health, welfare, and related problems. Its staff is drawn from four different municipal agencies: Welfare, Education, Probation, and the Youth Board. Its program is concerned with family service and neighbourhood improvement, and plans for an extensive research into the effect of its work with multi-problem families were published in June 1962.

In Bristol, England, in 1953 the Carnegie Trust sponsored a five-year action research project into juvenile delinquency, of which a report is now in the course of publication (Spencer et al., #41). The neighbourhoods chosen for this project included a new housing estate on the periphery of the city containing a high proportion of multi-problem families and juvenile delinquents.

These examples provide some evidence of one trend in the development of a co-ordinated range of services to multi-problem families on a neighbourhood basis.

Housing

Although there is general recognition of the harm done to family life through overcrowded housing and slum living, policies differ widely between Britain, Canada (#54), and the United States (#215) as to the appropriate level of public housing. In Britain, for example, nearly a quarter of the population now live in local authority houses. In spite of these differences in policy over the nature and extent of public provision, however, the multi-problem family presents difficult issues in housing management in most large cities in each country, since it is likely that low incomes, evictions from private housing, and arrears of rent will bring them to the attention of the responsible housing authority.

Three points deserve attention. The first is the importance of close relations between housing managers and workers in the health and welfare services. Multi-problem families are bad tenants and frequently in arrears of rent. They often cause trouble with neighbours and are destructive of property. Under such circumstances there is often strong pressure to evict them. In England the Ministry of Housing report on "Unsatisfactory Tenants" (#26) emphasized the damage to family life and to child welfare, as well as the cost of welfare services, through the break-up of families following eviction. The report also stressed the fact that the mere provision of a house was not usually enough, but that many of the 2,500 tenants evicted from council houses, as a result of eviction required skilled and persistent help over a considerable period of time. Such services are most useful only in the surroundings of an individual home.

The second point concerns the need for a pool of houses intermediate in standard between newly-built houses and those unfit for habitation. The "Unsatisfactory Tenants" report recommended the purchase by local authorities of older houses which, with some repair and redecoration, might be made habitable for a further period.

This proposal is closely linked with the third point -- the location of the multi-problem family. The writer of a recent study of multi-problem families in "Seaport" (Wilson, #49), strongly advocates a policy of dispersing the multi-problem family and of avoiding their segregation in groups living in close proximity to one another. The proposal is a controversial one: it is unrealistic in so far as it fails to take account of the intense hostility which many multi-problem families arouse in neighbours with different living standards. The report of the Bristol Project (#41) argues that some segregation of multi-problem families appears inevitable, but that it should be used as an opportunity for the planning of family casework and group work services for children and adolescents. The plan of intermediate accommodation recommended in "Unsatisfactory Tenants" carries with it, however, the great advantage that there might be some dispersal of multi-problem families in areas where the disparity between their own and their neighbours' standards might be relatively small.

Services for children and homemaker services

A variety of factors contribute to the need, now generally recognized in many large urban areas, for services which provide opportunities for recreation, activity, and remedial teaching for children and which give help and advice in household management. These factors include the size of the family, the age of the children, the dirt and poverty of living conditions, the frequent pregnancies, and the additional burden which inadequate fathers create for their wives.

Services for children, moreover, provide a useful bridge in the building of relationships between caseworker and mother. For the pre-school child the nursery school, and for the school child the evening play group, can both help to meet the emotional needs of children which the school is often ill-equipped to deal with. In groups of these kinds there is a useful role for voluntary workers in partnership with professional supervision.

More recently, increasing attention has been paid to new ways of helping the hard-to-reach adolescent, through detached workers and experimental clubs of various kinds. In the United States, for example, the work of the New York City Youth Board (#219, #220) is by now well known through its publications. In a smaller city, the Huntington-Gifford Project at Syracuse[32] points to the value of experimental work within the framework of a family centre, linked with a research program.

VI

Future Treatment and Research

It seems inevitable that there will always be a residual group of families whose behaviour continues to defeat the best efforts of workers both in practice and in research. Nevertheless, there have been important developments in understanding and in working with these families in the last twenty years. Also, there has gradually emerged a greater public awareness of their needs.

The early belief in a social problem group has given way to a more sensitive understanding of the growth of personality in childhood and its consequences for adult development. The original emphasis on the nature of the problems of the multi-problem family has shifted to the area of family diagnosis. There is general agreement that intensive family-centred casework, using more aggressive and less conventional methods than were accepted in the earlier literature, constitutes a fruitful approach to treatment.

The wide variety of projects already in existence or at the planning stage shows a readiness to experiment in different ways. Study of the social and cultural background of these families is beginning to achieve a place in the general approach to treatment. It is, however, essential to recognize, as Lukoff and Mencher (#301) argue the Community Research Associates have failed to appreciate, that social prophylaxis cannot be restricted to the family and primary groups but is closely related to much larger social units and the total structure of our society.

A great deal of work still remains to be done both in treatment and prevention as well as in research, and there must be the closest collaboration between practice and research. It is indeed a fair criticism of many of the existing projects that a clearly defined psychological and sociological framework, together with a research plan for the evaluation of treatment, is often lacking. The stage in multi-problem family work has now been reached when new knowledge will be gained only through collaboration of this kind.

Some of the more important future steps in understanding and treatment may be summarized as follows:

Diagnosis and Treatment

The most outstanding need is for improvement in family diagnosis and the extension of opportunities for treatment in depth. Alongside this is required a more sophisticated classification of family types and kinds of pathology associated with these types. There is need also of studies in the relationship between the personality of the individual family member and the family as a functioning group. Lastly, we need to identify more precisely different kinds of treatment required for different kinds of family, and to examine the nature of change and the areas in which change takes place as a result of treatment.

Intelligence

The level of intelligence in the multi-problem family is still a neglected question. Although the validity of many of the early studies of intelligence is now disputed, we still have little reliable data as the result of psychological testing and research. A great deal of the evidence comes from estimates made by workers in contact with the families. The effect of emotional retardation on poor intellectual performance is only vaguely known. Yet such knowledge is particularly necessary if the goals towards which the multi-problem family is helped to strive are to be realistic.

Social Class and Lower-Class Culture

Generally speaking, sociologists have done little research work with the multi-problem family. Our knowledge of the reference groups of these families remains vague and even contradictory. The evidence in favour of identification with lower-class standards is by no means clear. The distinction between real and nominal values made by Baldamus and Timms (#4) is indicative of the importance of research in this area. In what ways does the multi-problem family identify with middle-class values?

Research is also needed into the relationship between the multi-problem family and the kinship group, with friends and neighbours in different types of community, both rural and urban, as well as in different ethnic groups.

Planning and Co-ordination of Services

It is fair to say that we are still in what may be called the "project phase of development". As yet, no clear and uniform pattern of services has emerged. In the United States and Canada there is a wide variety of projects, largely un-co-ordinated with one another in operation. In Great Britain there is a greater measure of uniformity, partly as a result of the work of the Family Service Units and partly through Government intervention. In all countries, although there is general agreement on the difficulties created by multiplicity of visits to the family and by the overlapping of services, no clear pattern for the future has yet emerged.

In this report we have stressed the importance of experiment in the classification of different levels of treatment and different categories of worker. But we are by no means clear as to the precise roles to be played by each of the several health and welfare agencies.

Questions arise, such as: Should a single service or several services be involved? Where should the major responsibility for treatment lie? What are the most effective methods of co-ordination? To what extent should services be organized on a neighbourhood basis? The answers to these and similar questions will vary according to differences in political and administrative structure and in the availability of skill and resources.

Finally, there is need for the translation of professional understanding into simple language and straightforward ideas for the use of the large numbers of untrained and voluntary workers, both inside and outside the social services, whose experience with the multi-problem family sometimes results in bewilderment and anxiety.

References

1. Cf. Charles Booth, <u>Life and Labour of the People in London</u>, London: Macmillan and Company, 1903 (final volume).

2. <u>Report of the Mental Deficiency Committee (Wood Report)</u>, London: Her Majesty's Stationery Office, 1929 (especially Part III, Chapter V).

3. Numbers in parentheses refer to items in the Annotated Bibliography.

4. (in) *Proceedings of the British National Conference on Social Work* (The Family), National Council of Social Service, London, 1953.

5. "Max Siporin, in summarizing the work on the problem family, has made the cogent observation that present-day American social workers and sociologists, in contrast to our English colleagues, have preferred to concentrate on the process of family maladjustment rather than to focus on the stereotyping of families with the use of such epithets as hard-core, inadequate, and disordered."

6. Michael Argyle, "A New Approach to the Classification of Delinquents with Implications for Treatment," (in) *Kinds of Treatment for Kinds of Delinquents*, Board of Corrections, State of California, Sacramento, California, July 1961 (Monograph No. 2).

7. Charles Booth, *op. cit.*

8. C. R. Shaw, *Delinquency Areas*, Chicago: University of Chicago Press, 1929.

9. R. Faris, and H. W. Dunham, *Mental Disorders in Urban Areas*, Chicago: University of Chicago Press, 1939.

10. Terence Morris, *The Criminal Area*, London: Routledge and Kegan Paul, 1958.

11. Hermann Mannheim, *Juvenile Delinquency in an English Middletown*, London: Routledge and Kegan Paul, 1948.

12. J. C. Spencer, "Planning of a Social Project in Bristol," *Case Conference*, 1:3 (1954).

13. Howard Jones, "Approaches to an Ecological Study," *The British Journal of Delinquency*, 8:4 (April 1958), 277-293.

14. R. K. Merton, *Social Theory and Social Structure*, Glencoe, Ill.: The Free Press, 1957 (rev. ed.).

15. A. K. Cohen, *Delinquent Boys: The Culture of the Gang*, Glencoe, Ill.: The Free Press, 1955.

16. R. A. Cloward and L. E. Ohlin, *Delinquency and Opportunity*, Glencoe, Ill.: The Free Press, 1960.

17. R. Dahrendorf, *Class and Class Conflict in an Industrial Society*, London: Routledge and Kegan Paul, 1961.

18. B. M. Spinley, *The Deprived and the Privileged*, London: Routledge and Kegan Paul, 1953.

19. Lloyd Braithwaite, "Sociology and Demographic Research in the British Caribbean," *Social and Economic Studies*, 6:4 (1957).

20. Hyman Rodman, "On Understanding Lower-Class Behaviour," *Social and Economic Studies*, 8:4 (December 1959).

21. Madeline Kerr, *The People of Ship Street*, London: Routledge and Kegan Paul, 1958.

22. M. Young, and P. Willmott, *Family and Kinship in East London*, London: Routledge and Kegan Paul, 1957; Penguin Books, 1962.

23. E. Bott, *Family and Social Network*, London: Tavistock Publications, 1957.

24. Lee Rainwater et al., *Workingman's Wife*, New York: Oceana Publications, 1959.

25. Charles Booth, *op. cit.*, p. 207.

26. Alice Overton, "Casework as a Partnership," *Children*, 3:5 (1956).

27. *Report of the Committee on Children and*

Young Persons (Ingleby Committee), London: Her Majesty's Stationery Office, 1960, para. 46.

28. L. Rapaport, "The Concept of Prevention in Social Work," Social Work, 16:1 (1961).

29. Lukoff and Mencher (#301) are severely critical of the approach of Buell and the Community Research Associates for their rejection of the concept of prevention on the general public health model. They believe that a much broader definition than that advanced by C.R.A. is necessary: ". . . prevention and control of dependency implies a broad attack on the social and economic front and cannot be restricted to psychological inadequacies leading to dependency."

30. W. H. Beveridge, Social Insurance and Allied Services ("The Beveridge Report"), New York: The Macmillan Company, 1942. The capital letters were used by Beveridge.

31. Bradley Buell discusses these three C.R.A. projects in the article annotated under #125.

32. Norman R. Roth, Reaching the Hard-to-Reach (report on the Huntington-Gifford Project on Hard-to-Reach Youth), The Huntington Family Center, Inc., Syracuse, New York, July 1961.

COMMUNITY TREATMENT PROGRAMS
FOR MULTI-PROBLEM FAMILIES

Joseph C. Lagey
and
Beverly Ayres

Introduction

In 1962, the authors undertook a survey[1] of multi-problem family projects in all communities of 100,000 or over in North America. The purpose of this survey was twofold:

1. To report to an ad hoc committee on the number, types, and common problems of problem-family projects presently underway or in the planning stage. This committee was convened at the NASW Research Section's Annual Meeting at the 1960 National Conference on Social Welfare by research directors and others involved in multi-problem family projects for the purpose of establishing a "clearing house" on such projects. It was felt desirable to establish procedures whereby persons concerned with methodology, experimental design, treatment, and implementation of such projects could communicate with one another.

2. The second purpose was to obtain information which would be of use in planning for a multi-problem family project[2] which was then in the process of being developed.

Although this project was to be built upon the experience and findings of the Family-Centered Project of St. Paul, it was felt necessary to learn as much as possible of the various experiments in treatment which were being explored in other communities. The Neighborhood Improvement Project of New Haven, for example, which was also built upon the experience of the Family-Centered Project, had added intensive, reaching-out group work services to its treatment program. Other innovations, many of an exciting nature, were either underway or planned in the 143 communities reporting some phase of programing for problem families.

Treatment considerations were not the only concerns. From a research point of view several major problems were foreseen. The first was that of selecting a control group, which the pioneer project in St. Paul found under the then prevailing conditions unfeasible to establish. A corollary to this was control for "contamination" of both clients and treatment personnel who were to be assigned to the control group. Since a procedure for evaluating or rating client movement had been developed in St. Paul,[3] and refinements were presently being studied by Geismar and his collaborators at Rutgers, this was not seen as a major obstacle in setting up the methodology for an outcome study. What still remained a major research problem was how to account for, to separate out of any client movement, the "Hawthorne" or, as Blenkner has more appropriately stated it, the "placebo effect".[4]

What has emerged out of this survey is an indication that a considerable ferment is actively underway throughout almost every large community in North America. A wide range of projects has been reported upon, running the range from informal "difficult case committees" to formal joint case conferences, to casework-group work team approaches, to the massive, bold community organization projects being encouraged by the Ford Foundation. These are the settings in which the profession of social work has in part responded to the growing scrutiny, the reassessment of the effectiveness of the traditional efforts at ameliorating chronic dependency. While "Newburghitis" might capture public attention momentarily, there has been a remarkable response by both public and voluntary agencies, not on how to exercise more punitive controls on the "over consumers" of health and welfare resources, but how to rehabilitate such families and to explore ways in which the generation-to-generation bond may be severed.

The survey findings also show a serious deficiency in communication. Many communities are proceeding as if there had been no prior experience nor wisdom accumulated. There are projects underway where the likelihood of developing new knowledge and new methods of treatment can be seriously questioned. Research methodology is also woefully absent. The use of control groups is absent far more than it is present. Many projects are not using before-after designs. Very often little or no thought is given to evaluation of outcome.

On the basis of the preliminary analysis of the data, the findings do suggest the need for establishing some better means of communication. The concerns of the NASW Research Section's ad hoc committee appear to be justified. While it is desirable and encouraging that the spirit of experimentation is demonstrably so alive, much of this experimentation will have come to naught unless some more adequate strategy is worked out. If there is to be duplication of projects, let it be a planned replication. If measurement is to be employed, let it be a standardized instrument so that it will be possible to compare the effectiveness of different methods or procedures of treatment.

Abstracts of the 117 projects describing administrative structure, treatment procedures, and research design are presented in the complete report. The report also has full reference to written materials and the contact person for each community project.

Survey Results

Community welfare councils were selected for the initial phase of the survey, as it was felt that they were in the best position in most communities to know about local treatment programs for multi-problem families. The sample chosen for the initial questionnaire included all councils (or chests where there was no council) serving a population of 100,000 or more in Canada and the United States. Where a province or state had no city of this size the largest city was solicited; a few smaller communities were included where current information about a program had been obtained through other means. The total number of communities included was 260; 18 of these were in Canada.

In March 1962, an initial questionnaire was sent to councils asking if any special programs for multi-problem families were underway and, if so, the appropriate person to be contacted for further information. Second questionnaires went to these sources requesting more detailed information about various administrative, treatment, and research aspects of the programs, and for any written material available.

Of the 260 communities in the survey, first questionnaires were returned by 238, or a return rate of 91.5 per cent, which was most gratifying. Nearly all the non-respondents were from smaller cities, so that comprehensive coverage of major cities was not seriously impaired.

Of the 238 communities from which information was available, 95, or 39.9 per cent, reported that no special programs were underway locally. In the remaining 143 communities, or 60.1 per cent of those reporting, programing for multi-problem families was at some stage of thought, planning, or operation. This figure clearly indicates the extent of concern throughout the social welfare field about this group of families which are so costly in time and money.

There was a strong relationship between size of city and presence or absence of such programing, only 46 per cent of smaller communities (50,000 - 199,000) but 84 per cent of cities over 1,000,000 being so involved.

Programing in the 143 communities was further classified into two developmental phases:

Phase	Number Communities	Per Cent
Study, thought, early planning	67	46.9

Advanced planning, in operation or recently concluded	76	53.1
	143	100.0

The cutoff point of "Advanced Planning" was defined as programs with a fairly detailed design of project operation, whether or not financing had been obtained.

In the 76 communities in advanced developmental stage, a total of 117 different projects or programs was reported.

An analysis of the dominant treatment method of these programs suggested a broad classification into five types: (1) the case conference approach; (2) the intensive casework approach; (3) the multi-service approach, using various co-ordinated or integrated combinations of casework, group work, community organization, health and rehabilitation services; (4) the community development approach; and (5) other less common approaches.

Using this scheme and adding one further category of "could not be classified" (material not received), the 117 programs break down as follows:

Type	Number Programs	Per Cent
Could not be classified	9	7.7
Case conference	24	20.5
Intensive casework	44	37.6
Multi-service	20	17.1
Community development	16	13.7
Other	4	3.4
	117	100.0

The most popular approach at the present time is the intensive casework approach, which accounts for 38 per cent of the programs. If the classificatory scheme (<u>excepting</u> "other") is viewed as a kind of continuum from the simplest to the most complex, as well as from the oldest to the newest approach, historically, it might be projected that future developments in programs for problem families will show a heavier concentration in the multi-service and community development approaches. Descriptions of all the approaches are given below.

The Treatment Approaches

1. Case Conference Approach

This approach involves a presentation of material about a case from various members of a formally-assembled group, formulation of a group diagnosis and treatment plan, and assignment of responsibility for treatment (or parts of a treatment plan) to an agency (or agencies). It may include a follow-up of cases through periodic review, and assessment of results.

The most common type is the inter-agency case conference, made up of representatives of major community health and welfare agencies, both public and private, under the auspices of one organization, usually the local community welfare council. The group meets monthly to consider one or more multi-problem cases (sometimes called multi-agency cases), and there is no special financing or staffing. This kind of approach is often the first one taken in communities concerned about developing better services to problem families, as the association of agencies is a voluntary one and the program does not threaten agency autonomy or propose radical change in function, as do some of the approaches below.

2. Intensive Casework Approach

This approach emphasizes intensive family-centred casework, with co-ordination of other necessary services, by one special caseworker. One worker is assigned primary responsibility for each family and has a reduced caseload (12 to 35 families). A number of treatment techniques are used. There is an emphasis on "reaching out" to families, or "aggressive casework". This involves a stress on home visiting. The focus of the worker is on the whole family situation, with all members and all problems part of diagnostic and treatment planning. Particular effort is made to include fathers in treatment. The beginning point of work with the family is usually around the most evident and emergent needs, with stress on concrete services. The worker attempts to build a partnership relationship with the family, and seeks ways to enable them to "give back" to the community. The primary goal of treatment is the improvement of social functioning of the family, and on inter-personal ties, rather than on insight into intra-psychic functioning by individual members. The worker attempts to help the family form more positive relationships with community institutions and agencies and, as the primary treatment person, acts as a co-ordinator of other necessary health and welfare services.

The intensive casework approach is found under several administrative arrangements: (1) present agency structure is maintained, with each participating agency undertaking to provide one or more workers who give intensive casework to small loads of problem families (usually a central project staff serves to administer and co-ordinate the program); (2) a new department, or special unit, is set up in an existing agency or agencies, or the internal structure of an agency is altered; or (3) a new agency is created just to deal with multi-problem families.

3. <u>Multi-Service Approach</u>

In this approach an integrated treatment plan is used involving some combination of casework, group work, community (neighbourhood) organization, health and rehabilitation services. Casework provides family and individual counselling, with emphasis on family-centred casework techniques. A wide variety of programs may be offered through group work services, as recreation programs for individuals and families, nursery school, summer camping, after-school activities, discussion groups, therapeutic groups, parent education classes, clothing exchanges, detached youth work, etc. Through community or neighbourhood organization work is carried on with churches, schools, and neighbourhood groups, with an emphasis on improving the neighbourhood relationships of families. Attempts are made to help families become neighbourhood "strengtheners", a source of leadership and help for less adequate families.

This kind of integrated program is usually carried out in an area or neighbourhood and the activities are co-ordinated through the use of staff meetings, case conferences, etc. Some programs may also provide ancilliary health services, such as medical clinics or mental health clinics.

Various types of administrative structure are found: (1) one agency, usually a community or neighbourhood centre, operates the program; (2) a co-ordinated effort between two or more organizations, as a neighbourhood centre and a casework agency, or a centre and a public housing authority; (3) an integrated service combining under one administration the services of several organizations.

4. <u>Community Development Approach</u>

The newest development on the social service scene is the massive community development program which attempts to tackle areas of the central city ("gray areas") in which there is a high incidence of social pathology. The focus of many of these programs is on increasing opportunities for youth. These multi-faceted programs are directed at developing such things as: local leadership and participation, rehabilitation services for families and individuals, comprehensive recreation plans, economic upgrading both through employment opportunities and vocational training, environmental upgrading through urban renewal and environmental sanitation, improved educational opportunities, modification of racial attitudes, etc.

While these efforts are not specific to the multi-problem family, they recognize the presence of many such families. In a sense, these programs are as much designed to prevent and control some of the conditions which spawn multi-problem families as they are designed specifically to treat the problem family

5. <u>Other Approaches</u>

   a. <u>Volunteer Case Aide Programs</u>

   In this approach, selected volunteers visit problem families on a friendly visiting basis, with the purpose of helping families avoid crisis situations and make more effective use of other social services. Volunteers are carefully selected, trained, and supervised by social workers.

   b. <u>Homemaker-Housekeeper Programs</u>

   Special home helps or housekeepers visit families frequently, aid with cooking, cleaning, and child care and teach rudiments of housekeeping. Mothercraft and homemaking classes may be provided. Such programs are under social work or nursing supervision.

   c. <u>Residential Training Programs</u>

   In this approach, whole families or mothers and children are sent to a training centre for intensive rehabilitative treatment. Mothers are given instruction in housekeeping, child care, budgeting, etc., and fathers receive job training and help in securing employment. Other services may include group programs, health services, and counselling. This kind of approach has been used in England and the Netherlands, and was not included in the survey proper.

Listing of Communities and Programs

Below is an alphabetical listing of communities and programs. Only those programs in the advanced stage of planning or operation are included:

Community	Title of Program	Type
Ann Arbor, Michigan	Special Services Project	Intensive Casework
Atlanta, Georgia	Neighborhood rogram	Intensive Casework
Berkeley, California	Committee on Multi-Problem Families	Intensive Casework
Boston, Massachusetts	Chronic Problem Family Project	Intensive Casework
Boston, Massachusetts	Community Services Center	Multi-Service
Boston, Massachusetts	Action for Boston Community Development	Community Development
Burlington, Vermont	Client Referral Procedures Committee	Intensive Casework
Canton, Ohio	Community School Project	Community Development
Charleston, West Virginia	Inter-Agency Coordinating Group	Case Conference
Chicago, Illinois	Intensive Casework Service	Intensive Casework
Chicago, Illinois	Rockwell Gardens Demonstration Project	Multi-Service
Chicago, Illinois	Home Economics Program and Casework Program	Multi-Service
Chicago, Illinois	Pilot Project on Urbanization	Multi-Service
Cinncinnati, Ohio	Family Services Division	Intensive Casework
Cleveland, Ohio	Demonstration of the Application of Social Services in a Public Housing Estate	Multi-Service
Cleveland, Ohio	Hough Community Development Program	Community Development

Community	Title of Program	Type
Columbus, Ohio	Columbus Area Family Rehabilitation and Research Project	Intensive Casework
Corpus Christi, Texas	Program for Living	Intensive Casework
Dallas, Texas	Inter-Agency Project	Intensive Casework
Dayton, Ohio	Urban Renewal Program	Community Development
Decatur, Illinois	Case Conference Committee	Case Conference
Denver, Colorado	Juvenile Delinquency Control Program	Community Development
Detroit, Michigan	Brightmoor Family Service Consultation Project	Multi-Service
Detroit, Michigan	Social Service Cooperative Project	Multi-Service
Des Moines, Iowa	Woodward, Clarinda, Toledo Committees	Case Conference
Des Moines, Iowa	Polk County Youth Development Project	Intensive Casework
El Centro, California	Imperial County Health and Welfare Project	Multi-Service
Elkhart, Indiana	Pilot Youth Project	Intensive Casework
El Paso, Texas	Case Conference	Case Conference
Elmira, New York	Difficult Case Committee	Case Conference

Community	Title of Program	Type
Elmira, New York	Research Demonstration with Dependent Multi-Problem Families	Intensive Casework
Fort Wayne, Indiana	Inter-Agency Project	Intensive Casework
Glendale, California	Adult Case Conference Committee	Case Conference
Hagerstown, Maryland	Prevention and Control of Indigent Disability	Multi-Service
Hammond, Indiana	Difficult Case Conference	Case Conference
Harrisburg, Pennsylvania	Family Rehabilitation Program	Intensive Casework
Houston, Texas	Protective Services Project	Intensive Casework
Houston, Texas	Houston Housing Authority Project for ADC Families	Multi-Service
Houston, Texas	Homemaker Service Demonstration Project	Other
Houston, Texas	Neighborhood Development Program	Community Development
Indianapolis, Indiana	Haughville Multi-Problem Family Project	Case Conference
Indianapolis, Indiana	Three Year Demonstration in the Rehabilitation of Sixteen Families	Intensive Casework
Jackson, Michigan	Case Conferences	Case Conference
Knoxville, Tennessee	Cooperative Services Committee	Case Conference

Community	Title of Program	Type
London, Ontario	London Family Centred Project	Intensive Casework
Los Angeles, California	Rehabilitation-Training-Job Placement Demonstration Project	Intensive Casework
Los Angeles, California	Volunteer Friendly Visiting Services for Families	Other
Los Angeles, California	Youth Opportunity Board	Community Development
Middletown, Connecticut	Family Rehabilitation Program	Intensive Casework
New Britain, Connecticut	Sub-Committee on Hard to Reach Families	Case Conference
New Brunswick, New Jersey	Case Conference	Case Conference
New Haven, Connecticut	Neighborhood Improvement Project	Multi-Service
New Haven, Connecticut	Opportunities	Community Development
New York, New York	Special Family Counseling Unit	Intensive Casework
New York, New York	Referral Units Project	Intensive Casework
New York, New York	Tri-Agency Project	Intensive Casework
New York, New York	Interdepartmental Neighborhood Service Center	Multi-Service
New York, New York	Mental Health and Rehabilitation Demonstration Project	Multi-Service
New York, New York	East Harlem Demonstration	Community Development

Community	Title of Program	Type
New York, New York	Mobilization for Youth	Community Development
New York, New York	Community Action Program	Community Development
Newark, New Jersey	Human Renewal Program	Community Development
Newark, New Jersey	Project Hayes Homes	Multi-Service
Niagara Falls, New York	Special Unit	Intensive Casework
Oakland, California	Community Development Program	Community Development
Omaha, Nebraska	Family Rehabilitation Program	Intensive Casework
Ottawa, Ontario	Community Work Project for Multi-Problem Families	Intensive Casework
Pasadena, California	Case Conference Project	Case Conference
Peoria, Illinois	Case Conference Committee	Case Conference
Philadelphia, Pennsylvania	Rehabilitation Project	Intensive Casework
Philadelphia, Pennsylvania	Project Outreach	Intensive Casework
Philadelphia, Pennsylvania	Intensive Service Project	Intensive Casework
Philadelphia, Pennsylvania	Operation Poplar	Multi-Service
Philadelphia, Pennsylvania	Youth Conservation Services	Multi-Service
Philadelphia, Pennsylvania	Social Services Division	Other
Pittsburgh, Pennsylvania	Advisory Committee on Relocation Problems	Case Conference
Pittsburgh, Pennsylvania	Social Plan for Homewood-Brushton Area	Community Development

Community	Title of Program	Type
Portland, Maine	Special Aid to Dependent Children Project	Intensive Casework
Providence, Rhode Island	Community Renewal Program	Community Development
Reading, Pennsylvania	Rehabilitative Services Project	Intensive Casework
Richmond, Virginia	Special Aid to Dependent Children Units	Intensive Casework
Rochester, New York	Special Experiment with Multi-Problem Families	Intensive Casework
Rochester, New York	Volunteer Case Aide Program	Other
Rockford, Illinois	Case Conference Committee	Case Conference
St. Louis, Missouri	Case Conference Project	Case Conference
St. Louis, Missouri	Experimental Program with Multi-Problem Families	Intensive Casework
St. Louis, Missouri	Multi-Problem Family Project	Intensive Casework
St. Louis, Missouri	Pruitt-Igoe Demonstration Project	Intensive Casework
St. Paul, Minnesota	Family Centered Project	Intensive Casework
St. Paul, Minnesota	Work Reorientation Program	Intensive Casework
St. Petersburg, Florida	Multi-Problem Family Committee	Case Conference
Saginaw, Michigan	Youth Protective Services	Intensive Casework

Community	Title of Program	Type
San Francisco, California	Family Rehabilitation Program	Intensive Casework
San Mateo, California	Coordinating Bureau for Family Services	Intensive Casework
Schenectady, New York	Case Conference Program	Case Conference
Syracuse, New York	Family Consultation Service	Intensive Casework
Syracuse, New York	Multi-Service Project for Troubled Families	Multi-Service
Tampa, Florida	Inter-Agency Committee	Case Conference
Terre Haute, Indiana	Rehabilitation of Financially Dependent Families	Intensive Casework
Tulsa, Oklahoma	Difficult Case Committee	Case Conference
Utica, New York	Community Development Program	Community Development
Vancouver, British Columbia	Joint Family Services Project	Multi-Service
Vancouver, British Columbia	Area Demonstration Project	Multi-Service
Waco, Texas	Case Conference Committee	Case Conference
Washington, D.C.	Neighborhood Service Project	Multi-Service
Washington, Pennsylvania	Special Social Services	Intensive Casework
Wilmington, Delaware	Pilot Project for Rehabilitation of Dependent Families	Intensive Casework
Woodmere, Long Island, New York	(No title)	Intensive Casework

Could not be classified:

Chicago, Illinois	(Y.M.C.A.)
Cleveland, Ohio	(Merrick House)
Columbus, Georgia	(Public Welfare Department)
Elizabeth, New Jersey	(Council)
Philadelphia, Pennsylvania	(Experiment in Services to Children - Council)
Los Angeles, California	(Avalon Community Center)
Sydney, Nova Scotia	(Children's Aid Society)
Trois Rivieres, Quebec	(Centre de Service Social)
Tucson, Arizona	(Council)

References

1. Joseph C. Lagey and Beverly Ayres, *Community Treatment Programs for Multi-Problem Families*, Community Chest and Councils of the Greater Vancouver Area, Vancouver, B.C., December 1962.

2. "Area Demonstration Project," Community Chest and Councils of the Greater Vancouver Area, Vancouver, B.C., 1962.

3. L. L. Geismar and Beverly Ayres, *Measuring Family Functioning*, Family Centered Project, St. Paul, Minn., 1961.

4. Margaret Blenkner, "Control Groups and the Placebo Effect in Evaluative Research," *Social Work*, 7:1 (Jan. 1962), 52-58.

THE MULTI-PROBLEM FAMILY IN CANADA
A GLANCE BACKWARD IN 1970

Benjamin Schlesinger

There is increasing evidence that many of the parents of multi-problem families suffered considerable deprivation themselves during the early years of their lives. Many came from broken homes in which one parent, usually the father, had deserted or was imprisoned. Many, as children, had periods of institutional or foster-home placement or were brought up by a series of relatives. If they remained at home, their mothers were often employed and the children received inadequate substitute care. The mothers who had been deserted often entered into common-law relationships, sometimes bearing children by several men. In other words, the parents of the multi-problem family of today often have come from families that had similar characteristics. Case records show that the social behaviour of families sometimes extends through several generations.

The social milieu of many multi-problem families suggests the nature of their psychological problems. Because they suffer such severe deprivation, they develop negative and hostile attitudes. Also, since they are often subjected to rejection by the community, they tend to isolate themselves from their neighbours. The negative attitudes of the community toward these deprived families are likely to be heightened if the families belong to a race or culture different from the predominant one. Although people of minority groups are often subjected to rejection in our society, the rejection is more overt if their standards of living or conduct deviate markedly from those prevailing.

One of the chief characteristics of both

adults and children of multi-problem families is their lack of trust in others. They have few friends and little contact with social groups. They are mistrustful of neighbours, employers, physicians, nurses, school teachers, social workers, public officials, and so forth. In their dealings with health and welfare agencies they may express interest in the service offered, but they tend to avoid personal involvement, often failing to carry through on plans that have been worked out with them.

Because of their extreme distrust of people, members of these families have an exaggerated fear of authority. Most people, of course, have some fear of authoritative agencies, particularly courts or other official bodies. Members of disorganized families, however, have greater and more pervasive fear; they feel threatened even by persons who have limited legal authority and whose approach is non-authoritative. Schools, churches, and health and welfare agencies are not only the symbols of community mores and social standards; they also have certain powers that can be invoked.

Members of socially deprived families often have strong feelings of anger, aggression, and hostility intermingled with their mistrust and fear. Some are openly hostile and aggressive, while others attempt to hide their negative feelings behind a facade of friendliness and extreme politeness. Often these resentments go back to early childhood, when they were exposed to neglect, abuse, or abandonment by their parents. They have a sense of hopelessness which underlies all other feelings. They find temporary escape by going on a drinking or spending spree, by sexual promiscuity, by fighting, or by engaging in delinquent behaviour.

Any group of asocial clients will include some with various degrees of mental health. Some may have relatively little pathology; their deviant behaviour is largely a reaction to undue social strain and stress. Others may be psychotic or suffer from neurosis. A large proportion of asocial persons, however, fall into the category of "character disorders", the chief clinical feature of which is the arrest of the individual's emotional development. Because of inadequate parental care and guidance in early years, these people retain many infantile attitudes and ways of behaving. In consequence, their responses are more appropriate to the pre-school age of development than to the adult level. They have difficulty in deferring gratifications, have little judgment about money and other practical matters, are selfish and self-centred, and tend to get into trouble.

The definition used most widely in Canada for the multi-problem family is that a family is considered multi-problem if the following characteristics are present:

1. Failure in functioning of the father, such as alcoholism, criminal acts, desertion, mental illness, and the like.
2. Failure in functioning of the mother, such as alcoholism, criminal acts, desertion, mental illness, child neglect, and the like.
3. Failure in the functioning of the children, such as criminal acts, mental illness, poor school adjustment, and the like.
4. Failure in marital adjustment, such as out-of-wedlock children, promiscuity, severe marital discord.
5. Economic deprivation and grossly inadequate housing.
6. And as a result of three or more of the above-listed, the family has been a chronic or intermittent undue burden to a community for over three years.

This definition thus includes only families who have come to the attention of community agencies because of their many problems.

Identification of Multi-Problem Families

In our own capital, Ottawa, a small study of multi-problem families sheds some more light in this area.[1] In 1961, the Welfare Council of Ottawa surveyed a group of 47 multi-problem families. These were large families, averaging 7.2 members per family (Canadian average 3.5), and all lived in housing which was too costly, too crowded, or in poor physical condition. The education of the adults was limited to Grade 9 or less, and all were in debt and serious financial difficulty.

The families used 35 health and welfare agencies and had been known to one or another agency for 10 years or more. There was little co-ordination among the agencies, each agency serving the family not knowing what other agencies were doing with the particular family. Recommendations made in the report include co-ordination of services to these families.

Vancouver has pioneered in some pilot studies to identify and analyze multi-problem families in a metropolitan setting. In the month of June 1960, 1,407 multi-problem families, active with 14 social agencies, were identified in Vancouver. These families represented 21 per cent of agency case loads and were known by the agencies on an average of 4 years. The families seemed to live mostly in the downtown section, characterized by deteriorated housing, high land value, and low rentals. An interesting finding shows that these families were largely of Anglo-Saxon origin and had been residents of the city for generations. Vancouver estimated that about 12,000 to 16,000 people were involved with these families in the course of a year.

The Salter-Jarvis area in Winnipeg, which is approximately 5/8 of a mile in length and breadth, has a population of 3,000. In December 1962, 287 cases were being served in the area, the average-sized family being 3.5 members. It was estimated that 1,000 persons were in social or economic dependency, or both. Five agencies had been active in this area for many years but were showing little or no effect on the numerous and complex problems of these people. A large percentage of the 287 cases seemed to be families of the multi-problem type, since they were known by at least 2 to 4 agencies which were simultaneously extending services.

Halifax, Nova Scotia, identified 262 multi-problem families in 1966.

Two-Generation Problem Families

The study of two-generation families was undertaken in two social agencies in Metropolitan Toronto and covered 25 two-generation families, or 50 families.[2] The study revealed a much larger size family in this group of two-generation families than the average Canadian family: the average size in the first generation was 7.2, and in the second generation, 5.3. Most of the second-generation families were still active with social agencies in Toronto.

The two-generation families were confronted by a frightening array of problems, including alcoholism, illegitimacy, marital discord, ill-health, unemployment, delinquency and crime, housing, financial problems, and sexual deviation. There were also pronounced problems in the area of care and training of children. Child neglect in the forms of physical abuse, lack of health supervision, lack of parental control and guidance, illegitimacy, and desertion were present in most cases.

The problems that stood out sharply in the first generation were those of delinquency and crime, neglect, and lack of parental control of the children. In the second generation the most frequent problem was that of unmarried motherhood and illegitimacy.

The study also revealed that two-generation families are mainly located in the downtown section of the city of Toronto, where there is a heavy population concentration. Residential mobility was high in these families, with an average move per family of more than once a year, but largely within the same social milieu.

The data revealed that a high percentage of the children were cared for by social agencies. In the total number of families of both generations, 57.7 per cent of the children were placed with Children's Aid Societies. In addition, in both generations, 38.7 per cent of the children were placed by other means than Children's Aid Societies.

The average number of years a family was served by social agencies in the first generation was 7.2, and in the second generation, 3.8. Many of the problems confronting these families had come to the attention of a number of different health and welfare agencies in Metropolitan Toronto and outside of Toronto.

What emerged from this study was the prospect that if no concerted effort is made in an organized manner to prevent further dependency, the pattern of these families will continue from generation to generation.

Financial Costs

Another study calculated the costs for two Toronto multi-problem families.[3] Family "A" had been receiving help from 16 agencies over a period

of 17 years at a cost of $53,225, and Family "B",
known for 25 years, had used up $61,700 of public
and private funds. These costs did not include
the price paid in human terms by these families,
or the cost of services of the array of professional volunteer workers who had been in contact
with them.

Values of Multi-Problem Families

A study which examined the values of multi-problem families in London, Ontario, found that
there is considerable evidence that these people
do have a desire for change.[4] On the whole, they
are not satisfied with their lives as they are
living them. They largely identify with middle-class standards, which they see as desirable, but
which they have been frustrated in achieving. In
some instances, secondary problems are created by
their recognition of failure to achieve the expected. They feel that they are maintaining as
good standards as possible, although they are not
always satisfied with these. When they are criticized by the dominant middle-class society
(through the social worker, public health nurse,
etc.), their problems are reinforced rather than
alleviated, and they feel their difficulties and
differences all the more strongly. Thus, in some
cases, apparent lower-class behaviour does not
result from their identification with the lower
class but from their frustration in achieving more.

The families in London were still predominantly fertile, with the age range of the men from
21 to 45, and the women, 21 to 35. The average
number of children was 4.5, smaller than the average in other studies, which is usually 6. However,
this group was younger and still growing. That
23.3 per cent of the families had children under
6 years of age demonstrates the need for effective
and preventive measures. The greater percentage
of the sample were native-born. The occupations
of the male heads all required less education than

higher-paying jobs. These families would presumably become increasingly dependent economically as technological advances continue. Of the men, 46.6 per cent had an intermittent pattern of employment, 30 per cent a steady pattern, and 16.6 per cent were usually unemployed. Agency records in most cases were incomplete as far as education of the clients was concerned. In the 24 cases where education was recorded, none had schooling past Grade 12. Each family was known to an average of 6.1 of the 12 agencies from whom data were obtained. The average contact was 12.2 years from the date of the first contact to the date of the research.

Completed Projects Related to Multi-Problem Families

Vancouver. A study of 100 multi-problem families found that the most characteristic failure of the families was the inability to remain economically independent.[5] Ninety-five families had been in receipt of financial assistance for a period of one month or more. Twelve families were in receipt of assistance by the end of their first year of marriage, and some 34 families by the end of their fifth year of marriage.

Eighty-three of the families were characterized by "a dismemberment of conjugal pair". The first time dismemberment occurred, husbands left home in 59 cases and wives in another 24 cases. Thirty-four families, or 41 per cent of those broken by the absence of a spouse, experienced a second separation. A third separation was recorded for 7 families.

Fourteen per cent of first separations were in the category "multiple absences from the home situation" -- situations where there was a multiplicity of indefinite desertions which could not be tied down to specific periods of time but were judged to be sufficiently serious to constitute marital breakdown of the same order as a definite and prolonged absence from the home. Of the remaining 71 first separations, only 5 were enacted through formal channels of legal separation or divorce. Forty-five per cent represented desertion and 46 per cent separation by mutual agreement.

A mental health problem of the husband was recorded in 63 of the families, compared with a recording in this category for the wife in only 37 instances. Seventy-six per cent of the mental health problems of the husbands, and 22 percent of those of the wives, were classified as personality defect and social maladjustment.

Finally, only 23 per cent of the sample did not have contact with Family Court.

The sequence of failure in family functioning began approximately 6 years after marriage with a mental health problem of the husband. This was experienced by 63 of the families. However, 76 per cent of the husbands' problems were associated with alcoholism or heavy drinking.

These families found their experience of family casework under the project a considerable improvement over usual agency services. Owing largely to a combination of administrative factors, e.g., the worker remained active for three years and had small caseloads which enabled him to devote more time to his clients, the workers came to be considered as friends whom their clients could call on whenever they needed, and some families felt that their family relationships had improved as a result. Certainly it was a more pleasant experience; they were better able to find their way through the maze of agency regulations. However, there were limitations to what the worker could do for them in relation to the various institutions with which they had to deal. The worker could not alter the practices of Family Court, which many of the women felt favoured husbands who deserted their wives. They could not increase the size of the social assistance grant to what they would consider an adequate amount, or obtain jobs when there were none available. In short, from a limited storehouse of inadequate resources, the workers could only point out what was available.

<u>London (Ontario)</u>. London's population of 170,000 can boast one of the highest per capita incomes in Canada. A survey in 1959 indicated that 250 multi-problem families could be identified in that city. A Family-Centred Project, using the "intensive casework method", was begun in 1963 and completed in 1966. Final results of the study are based on data from 40 of these families selected for intensive service and 40 "control" families not receiving the service.[6]

The characteristics of the 40 families in the "experimental" group included the following: 40 per cent were headed by one parent, usually a mother whose husband was not likely to return; 80 per cent rented an apartment or a house; 21 per cent of the male heads were employed full time; 60 per cent of the families had a weekly income of $60. All families had a large number of children (40 per cent had 7 or more), many of these children by a number of different natural parents. The average number of children living at home was 4.4. Sixteen of the families had parents who were married to each other and living at home.

One caseworker was responsible for the work with all the members of a family and responsive to their problems in the various areas of social functioning. No provision was made for family group counselling or for the services of a treatment team. The worker took responsibility for implementing and co-ordinating the different services being provided to the family by the various social agencies involved in their welfare. This approach avoided the multitude of workers and agencies frequently found working with a multi-problem family without one agency's knowing about another agency's involvement.

Despite the heavy investment of manpower, service, money, and new approaches, the incidence of improvement in overall functioning in the experimental group was only slightly greater than in the control group. There were no cases in either group which achieved an "adequate" level of overall functioning by the end of the service. Family heads in the experimental group, however, evidenced improvement in their role as breadwinner. It may be a coincidence that an American study of multi-problem families in Elmira, New York, reported after two years of intensive service and great financial expenditure that "taking research as well as casework factors into consideration, an ultra-objective statement might be that whatever was done by these trained caseworkers, under these conditions and in this setting, cannot be demonstrated, on the basis of the particular measures we chose to apply, to have had an appreciable effect."[7]

Conclusion

We have yet to learn how to deal most effectively with this type of family. The London project is one part of Canada's efforts underway in Halifax, Montreal, Ottawa, Toronto, Winnipeg, and Vancouver to find out first the characteristics of the families, and then to attempt to intervene in the generational dependency pattern of these families, who represent only a small percentage of families in Canada and yet consume nearly half of the total welfare budgets of our metropolitan areas. The London experiment is only a beginning and points to further investigations. What stands out is that social workers alone cannot solve the problem of these families. More than part-time efforts are needed on their behalf. The total community will have to find ways to break the generational cycle of misery. At the same time it must be recognized that there are families for whom no concentrated efforts will be of avail, and they may have to be sustained for the rest of their lifetime. Hopefully, their children can be helped to emerge from the pattern of hopelessness and despair.

There are many areas related to the multi-problem family that have to be examined so that society may take the necessary preventive and social action. As of the present, however, there is no systematic inquiry into etiological or causal factors. No systematic studies have been directed at describing the general intellectual level, psychiatric impairment, or specific medical disability of this group. As yet we cannot answer the question raised earlier in the century as to whether or not these people are intellectually adequate. We do have some knowledge that indicates that they are poor school performers, that they have a high drop-out rate from schools, and that they are usually lacking in occupational skills. Despite these general observations it would be unsafe to state, until proven otherwise, that the families making up this 4 to 6 per cent who seem to remain in difficulty are intellectually inferior.

In a similar way, psychiatric disability appears to be present in an above-average proportion. But again there is no systematically presented body of observations or measures.

Although it is true that multi-problem families receive the most attention from the community, it is not true that they receive the most or even a fair share of its benefits. The basic responsibility for improving the lives of all Canadians rests with the community -- its people, institutions, and all else that make up the society in which we live. Every aspect of our lives is shaped and determined by the expectations of the society around us, whether it be family, school, job, or friends. This being so, it is our total society that must build a structure and provide an atmosphere that will assure the basic requirements necessary for the welfare of its members. Such things as good housing, adequate schools, education and vocational opportunities, absence of discrimination, health and medical programs -- all must be provided before we can judge any group of people to be "hard to reach", "hard core", or "self defeating".

References

1. Welfare Council of Ottawa, Multi-Problem Families, 1961.

2. E. Cameron, P. Chatterjee, E. Edmison, J. Robinson, and M. Sharpe, "An Exploratory Study of Two Generation Cases Serviced by Two Children's Aid Societies in Metropolitan Toronto", MSW Thesis, School of Social Work, University of Toronto, 1962.

3. Renee Roseman, "Two Hard Core Families", MSW Thesis, School of Social Work, University of Toronto, 1960.

4. J. Cheow, P. Gendron, B. Horsham, and B. Veitch, "The Values of the Multi-Problem Family", MSW Thesis, School of Social Work, University of Toronto, 1962.

5. United Community Services, Vancouver, The Area Development Project, 1969 (3 vols.).

6. United Community Services, London, Ontario, The Family-Centred Project, 1967.

7. David Wallace, "The Chemung County Evaluation of Casework Service to Dependent Multiproblem Families: Another Problem Outcome", Social Service Review, XLI (December 1967), 389.

BIBLIOGRAPHY

JOURNAL ABBREVIATIONS

Amer. J. Orthopsychiat. - American Journal of Orthopsychiatry
Amer. J. Pub. Health - American Journal of Public Health
Brit. J. Del. - British Journal of Delinquency
Brit. J. Psychiat. Soc. Wk. - British Journal of Psychiatric Social Work
Brit. J. Sociol. - British Journal of Sociology
Can. Welf. - Canadian Welfare
Case Conf. - Case Conference
Child Welf. - Child Welfare
J. Amer. Academy of Child Psychiat. - Journal of American Academy of Child Psychiatry
J. for Study of Interp. Processes - Journal for the Study of Interpersonal Processes
J. Housing - Journal of Housing
J. of Nervous and Mental Disease - Journal of Nervous and Mental Disease
J. Pub. Health - Journal of Public Health
J. Soc. Wk. Process - Journal of Social Work Process
Marr. Fam. Living - Marriage and Family Living
Pub. Welf. - Public Welfare
Quart. Rev. - Quarterly Review
Soc. Casewk. - Social Casework (U.S.A.)
Soc. Serv. - Social Service (British)
Soc. Wk. - Social Work (U.S.A.)
Soc. Worker - Social Worker (Canada)

OTHER ABBREVIATIONS

C.C. - Community Council
C.C.C. - Community Chest and Council
C.R.A. - Community Research Associates
C.S.W.E. - Council on Social Work Education
F.C.P. - Family-Centered Project
F.S.A. - Family Service Association
F.S.U. - Family Service Units
I.S.T.D. - Institute for the Study and Treatment of Delinquency
m.p. - multi-problem family
V.C.A. - Volunteer Case Aide Project

AUSTRALIA

1. VICTORIAN COUNCIL OF SOCIAL SERVICE, <u>Seminar on Multi-Problem Families in Our Victorian Community</u>, Victorian Council of Social Service, Melbourne, 1959, 44 pp.

    The report of the seminar contains four papers. The first deals with the Australian definition of the problem family and discusses the social services which are related to the problem family. The second paper covers the characteristics of 56 problem families, serviced by the Brotherhood of St. Laurence, and discusses the effects on husband, wife, and children. Health services are covered in the third paper, and the fourth discusses the Child Welfare Act of 1958 in relation to its limitations and coverage for m.p. families.

2. ---------, <u>How 56 Low Income Families Live</u>, Victorian Council of Social Service, Melbourne, 1962, 39 pp.

    A study of the budgets of 56 problem families in Melbourne. The distribution of income in the areas of food, clothing, health, and debts is presented, and the composition of these families is discussed. The report contains an appendix which describes in length five of the problem families in Australia.

B R I T A I N

3. A. R. H. F., "A Problem Family at School," Case Conf., 4:6 (Nov. 1957), 164-165.
    A case history of a problem family with school-age children, showing the reaction of school authorities to the difficult school behaviour.

4. BALDAMUS, W., and TIMMS, Noel, "The Problem Family: A Sociological Approach," Brit. J. Sociol., 6:4 (Dec. 1955), 318-326.
    The main purpose of the study is to find a theoretically-based methodological alternative to the biological-genetic approach in sociological research into problem families.

5. BARCLAY, Irene T., "Problem Families," Soc. Serv., (Sept.-Dec. 1951), 62-65.
    A survey of current research work in England on problem families. Briefly reported are: (1) five pilot surveys in Bristol, Luton, Rotherham, West Riding, Kensington, by the Problem Families Committee; the paper "Problem Families in Bristol" (Wofinden) is discussed; (2) an intensive survey of 66 problem families in Manchester, Salford, Oldham, by the Family Service Units; and (3) an intensive survey of 10 London problem families by the author. Discussing findings from the above, the author raises questions relevant to further research.

6. BASTIAANS, J., "Social Aspects of Slum Clearance, Rehousing and Redevelopment," Social Welfare Department, Rotterdam, Apr. 1957, 26 pp. (mimeo.).
    Report by a Dutch social worker on a study trip in England. He discusses his observations on slum clearance projects, problems of transition, new neighbours, and town planning. Housing for problem families is also included.

7. BLACKER, C. P. (ed.), <u>Problem Families: Five Inquiries</u>, Eugenics Society, London, 1952, 123 pp.
   The Eugenics Society was asked to do a study of 379 problem families in five different areas of England. The report includes an excellent history of the background of problem families, and discusses the characteristics of the sample in detail. Thirty-five case histories of problem families are reviewed, and the appendix contains the research documents used in the study.

8. BODMAN, Frank, "Personal Factors in the Problem Family," <u>Case Conf.</u>, 5:4 (Sept. 1958), 99-104.
   A sociological and theoretical look at problem families; included are the views of Karl Marx and Margaret Mead. The author also brings in cross cultural examples to show that we always had deviant behaviour in families.

9. BOOTH, Charles, <u>Life and Labour of the People in London</u>, London: Macmillan Co., Vol. I (Poverty), 1904, 324 pp.
   We find a good description of the problem family in this classic study in London, England. Booth discusses the characteristics of the problem family in vivid detail. It is well to remember that the m.p. family is not a recent phenomena in the social welfare area.

10. BRISKIN, Sidney I., "Who Are The Problem Families?," <u>Case Conf.</u>, 8:5 (Oct. 1961), 126-128.
    An article concerning problems of definition and description of "problem" families.

11. COOKSON, J. S., "Problem Families - A Follow-up," <u>Royal Society of Health Journal</u>, 82:3 (May-June 1962), 170-172.
    The author, who is county medical officer of Herefordshire, discusses a method of evaluating problem families prior to intensive service. He uses a scoring method, which takes into consideration standards of child

care, budgeting, cooking, cleanliness, clothing, and family relationships. The author proves, by using problem families in his county, that "much time might be saved by concentrating all energies on families which, at the start, show potential possibilities of improvement". He also adds that if no signs of improvement were evident, routine care would be indicated.

12. DONNISON, David, "The Problem of the Problem Family," Case Conf., 3:10 (Apr. 1957), 308-309.
    A critical review of the book by Philp and Timms (#28) on the problem family. The author feels that the term "problem family" is misleading and should be abandoned altogether.

13. FAMILY SERVICE UNITS, Annual Report 1960-61, Family Service Units, London, 20 pp.
    This report as well as previous ones gives an excellent picture of the work of the F.S.U. with problem families. There are presently 15 units in England, working on a comparatively small budget, with a field staff of approximately 70-75 full-time caseworkers. The F.S.U. is used for student training in social service work. The report is well illustrated with problem family case material. Agencies may well want to read these reports, as examples of good report writing and interpretation.

14. INSTITUTE FOR THE STUDY AND TREATMENT OF DELINQUENCY, The Problem Family - Four Lectures, I. S. T. D., London, 1958, 40 pp.
    Four lectures which include the topics of the Problem Family in Court, Personality Factors, Social Services, and the Problem Family. Some of the lectures are illustrated by case histories.

15. INSTITUTE (THE) OF HOUSING, The Problem of Unsatisfactory Tenants and Applicants, The Institute of Housing, London, June 1955, 8 pp.

Discussion of the difficulties faced by problem families in housing projects. The pamphlet outlines the various types of behaviour which tend to result in evictions and unsatisfactory tenants.

16. IRVINE, Elizabeth E., "Problem Families: A Discussion of Research Methods," Brit. J. Psychiat. Soc. Wk., 9 (May 1954), 24-33.
    The author stresses the great need for accurate diagnostic and psycho-pathological studies in the context of therapeutic casework with problem families. The article includes a survey of existing theories of aetiology, and discusses the methods of research into aetiology. The author recommends a warm permissive and supportive work approach to the "immature unresponsive" problem families.

17. --------, "Some Notes on Problem Families and Immaturity," Case Conf., 6:9 (Mar. 1960), 225-228.
    The author claims to have introduced the concept of "immaturity" in problem families. She criticizes Harriett Wilson's article (#48), and feels that the questions posed about immaturity have not been answered.

18. JOINT UNIVERSITY COUNCIL FOR SOCIAL STUDIES AND PUBLIC ADMINISTRATION, ENGLAND, "The X Case (Case Study No. 1), 1946-1950," Joint University Council for Social Studies and Public Administration, London, 50 pp. (private circulation).
    This is a five-year record of "an attempt made by a group of social caseworkers to rehabilitate a family" suffering from multiple problems. Each of the caseworkers was a specialist in his field. The work with the family was done on a co-operative basis by the whole group, and all participated in the group discussions, which were concerned with various aspects of the case.

19. JONES, D. Caradog, The Social Problem Group, Cambridge: Squire Law Library, Old Schools, 1945, 50 pp.

A discussion of poverty and basic costs of living. The author also includes a section on mental poverty and discusses intelligence in relation to problem families. There appears to be great emphasis on the aspect of low intelligence and its relation to problem families.

20. JONES, David, "The Prevention of Break-Up of Families," *Royal Society of Health Journal*, 76:2 (June 1956), 285-290.
    An interesting review of the work of the Family Service Units in England, with a case illustration. The author stresses the realistic casework approach to problem families used by the Family Service Units.

21. --------, "Family Service Units, England," *Can. Welf.*, 34:1 (May 1958), 19-23.
    A description of one of the approaches to problem families in Britain, through the Family Service Units, a voluntary casework agency with branches in 12 English towns.

22. LASSELL, Margaret, *Wellington Road*, London: Routledge and Kegan Paul, 1960, 159 pp.
    The author, who lived as a lodger with a typical problem family and kept a day-by-day record of the lives and problems of the members, gives here a detailed account of her experience.

23. LONDON COUNTY COUNCIL, "Problem Families - Employment of Social Workers," London County Council Health Committee, London, 1959, 6 pp. (mimeo.).
    A working document, which describes the need for using social workers in work with problem families.

24. MIDDLEMORE HOMES, "Crowley House, Family Rehabilitation Centre," Crowley House, Birmingham, 1959, 7 pp. (mimeo.).
    The house is set up to meet needs of problem families who are already receiving social work help. The environment of the house caters

to the needs of all the family members. The article describes the setting, staff, routine, and methods of work at the house. There is also a follow-up program. The average stay per family appears to be about 4 months.

25. ---------, Eighty-Fourth Report, Middlemore Homes, Birmingham, 1961, 16 pp.
    This organization administers two centres for problem families. The first is Crowley House, where mothers and their children spend from one to four months in residence. The other is at Lee Crescent, where furnished flats are available for families who need rehabilitation, and stay there for six months to two years. Details are available from the Middlemore Homes.

26. MINISTRY OF HOUSING, Unsatisfactory Tenants, London: Her Majesty's Stationery Office, 1955, 32 pp.
    Sixth report of the Housing Management Committee, which reviews the problem of unsatisfactory tenants in detail. It contains a summary of the work of public and private agencies concerned, and co-ordination of services is suggested. It is estimated that 2,500 tenants leave the public housing projects annually because they are asked to leave. Special accommodation for these problem families is recommended. The recommendations made by the committee centre on keeping problem families together.

27. M.L.D., "From Dependence to Independence: A Case Study," Case Conf., 4:8 (Feb. 1958), 233-236.
    A case study of a "problem" family taken from the files of the Family Service Units in Britain to illustrate change from dependence to independence through casework help.

28. PHILP, A. F., and TIMMS, Noel, The Problem of the Problem Family, Family Service Units, London, 1957, 77 pp.
    A critical survey of the literature on

"problem families". The book includes an analysis of descriptions and definitions of the problem family, and a contrast of two approaches to the subject found in the literature; also a survey of the literature on attempts to deal with problem families, and a brief analysis of ideas about research in the field. The book contains a bibliography of 154 items.

29. PHILP, A. F., <u>Family Failure: A Study of 129 Families with Multiple Problems</u>, London: Faber and Faber Ltd. (to be published in 1963).

This book is based on research which was undertaken by Douglas Woodhouse. A note from the publisher says, "Mr. Woodhouse, a psychiatric social worker, studied a number of problem families who have been helped by Family Service Units and the problems have been broken down into subjects such as money, earning and management, the health of the parents and their intelligence, marital relationships, contact with the law, and the care and treatment of children. A number of case histories give a vivid picture of the vicious circle in which a problem family lives and the support and help it needs over the years until some chord is touched which enables it to find strength in itself to resolve its own problems".

30. SAVAGE, S. W., "Intelligence and Infant Mortality in Problem Families," British Medical Journal, Jan. 19, 1946, 86-88.

    An attempt to look at intelligence and infant mortality of problem families. The author, who was at that time medical officer at Herefordshire, found 89 problem families in a population of 90,800. His findings indicate that only 29.2 per cent of mothers of problem families were found to be intellectually defective and consequently ineducable. The children were found to be retarded in school, and infant mortality was related directly to intelligence of mothers, being highest where intelligence was lowest.

31. ————————, "Rehabilitation of Problem Families," The Medical Officer, 75:26 (June 29, 1946), 252-253.

    Discussion of 89 problem families found in Herefordshire. Of the mothers, 30 per cent were found to be intellectually defective; the other 70 per cent are described as "educable". The author describes methods of helping educable problem families, and feels that it is not possible to reclaim the families where the mother is mentally defective.

32. SCOTT, J. A., "Appendix" on Problem Families in London, London County Council, Public Health Department, London, 1956, 36 pp. (see also Lancet, Jan. 25, 1958, 204-208).

    This appendix is part of the 1956 Annual Report of the Medical Officer of Health and Principal School Medical Officer of London County. The author reviews the social legislation, needs, family casework, methods of co-ordination and available services to problem families. The report discusses a problem family survey, which discovered 3,022 potential and hard-core problem families in London County. The Public Health Department then made an analysis of 1,000 of these families, and statistical data is given about this part of the survey. The appendix contains four "annexes", which summarize agencies involved with the families and give sample case histories. This is a model report on problem families, and has gathered much useful information within its pages.

33. --------, "Problem Families in London," The Medical Officer, 100 (Aug. 1958), 83-86.
A survey made by the Health Department of the London County Council, of problem families in London. Statistical data illustrate the findings of this survey, which estimates that London has 3,022 multi-problem families. The article is well illustrated with ten tables of figures containing such data as factors found in problem families, services available to them, and many other pertinent facts.

34. SHERIDAN, Mary D., "The Intelligence of 100 Neglectful Mothers," British Medical Journal, Jan. 14, 1956, 91-93.
A survey of 100 mothers who came from problem families and had been charged with "wilful neglect" of their children. The findings indicate that 70 of the mothers fell into the retarded group. The author concludes that the problem of the neglectful mother is primarily a medico-social rather than a penological one.

35. --------, "Neglectful Mothers," Lancet (Apr. 14, 1959), 722-725.
A follow-up study of 100 mothers who had been placed on probation and admitted to residential training homes after court appearances for child neglect. The author describes the characteristics of the mothers, fathers, and children and evaluates the results of the training in the residential homes. Early recognition and prevention is stressed, and it is pointed out that some problem families are just incurable.

36. SILVERMAN, Abner D., "The Rehabilitation of Problem Families," Housing Newsletter, 4:6 (Dec. 1960), 6-8.
A shorter digest of the material presented in annotation #37. The article is in a

Canadian journal of housing, published by the Ontario Department of Planning and Development.

37. ---------, "Problem Families - Efforts at Social Rehabilitation Yield Results in Britain," J. Housing, 18:2 (Feb. 1961), 63-70.
    An American Public Housing Administrator discusses the British approach to housing for the problem family. He reviews the various methods and projects in England, including London County Council and the voluntary social services which aid the problem families. He outlines the underlying basic British principles in working with these families. The article also includes references to American public housing projects for the problem family.

38. SMITH, Malcolm A., "Supplementary Report on Supervised Tenants," Burgh Factor, Paisley, Scotland, 1957, 4 pp. (mimeo.).
    A brief summary of schemes operated in England and Holland in relation to housing for problem families. The summary includes 10 projects in England and one in Holland.

39. ---------, "Housing Management," Housing, 22:1 (June 1960), 4-10.
    This article on housing management in Scotland includes a section on the current "Paisley Experiment" in Paisley, Scotland. The experiment includes close supervision of problem families in "supervised housing". The author cites facts and figures to indicate improvement, and indicates that in the future social workers will do intensive casework with these problem families.

40. ---------, "Supervision of Unsatisfactory Tenants," Burgh Factor, Paisley, Scotland, 1962, 6 pp. (mimeo.).
    A description of a housing project for "incorrigible" tenants. The paper reviews the scheme of supervision and summarizes

briefly the approach used in this project. Out of 210 families, 145 improved sufficiently to avoid further supervision, and only 10 families had to be ejected.

41. SPENCER, John C., in collaboration with DENNIS, N., and TUXFORD, Joy, <u>Stress and Release in an Urban Estate</u>, London: Tavistock Publications (publication expected in 1963).
This book is an abbreviated version of the report of the Bristol Social Project (England) presented to the Carnegie United Kingdom Trust. It is an account of an action research project concerned with family and neighbourhood life in two housing estates of an English city. Chapter 14 examines the ecology of the symptoms of "stress and strain". Fourteen problem families were included in the list of symptoms studied. The initial focus of this project was juvenile delinquency. The authors discuss the significance of a noticeable clustering of these symptoms in certain areas of the city, one of which was the urban estate in which the project was located. In Part 5 certain recommendations relating to social work training and method are suggested.

42. STALLYBRASS, C. O., "Problem Families," <u>The Medical Officer</u>, 75:10 (Mar. 9, 1946), 89-92.
An address delivered to the Liverpool Council of Social Service. The author reviews the historical development of the "submerged tenth" or problem families, and discusses prevention and rehabilitation measures.

43. STEPHENS, Tom (ed.), <u>Problem Families: An Experiment in Social Rehabilitation</u>, Pacifist Service Units, Liverpool, 1947, 72 pp.
A project report of an experiment carried out by three small groups of voluntary workers with problem families. The methods

used included casework, manual work, material aid, social and domestic education, co-operation with other agencies, and rehabilitation.

44. TIMMS, Noel, "Problem Family Supporters," Case Conf., 1:7 (Nov. 1954), 28-31.
    The author discusses material relief as part of casework policy with problem families. He presents case situations in one particular family, which illustrate demands made on the caseworker for support in material terms.

45. WARHAM, Joyce, and McKAY, Sheila, "Working with the Problem Family," Social Work, 16:4 (Oct. 1959), 126-132.
    A discussion of treatment and prevention in work with the problem family.

46. WILLSON, F. M. G., Administrators in Action, Toronto: University of Toronto Press, 1961, 350 pp. (especially Chapter 5).
    This book contains British case histories in administration. Chapter 5 contains a very good case which deals with a problem family, in which 8 agencies and 12 other interested parties are involved. The author discusses the background of the family, their problems, and how the multitude of agencies got involved in the case. The co-ordinating conference is discussed. This is an excellent case to illustrate the "problem of the problem family" and would be very helpful for teaching purposes.

47. WILSON, Harriett C., "Juvenile Delinquency in Problem Families in Cardiff," Brit. J. Del., 9:2 (Oct. 1958), 94-105.
    The experimental group consisted of 110 problem families. Boys only were considered in this study. The author examines the categories of juvenile delinquency which are prevalent among boys of problem families.

48. ---------, "Problem Families and the Concept of Immaturity," Case Conf., 6:5 (Oct. 1959), 115-118.
    A discussion of the concept of "immaturity"

on the basis of an examination of case material of 157 problem families in Cardiff. The term "immaturity" is defined, and the question whether it is related only to problem families is examined.

49. --------, Delinquency and Child Neglect, London: George Allen and Unwin Ltd., 1962, 208 pp.
A comprehensive study of a group of problem families in England. The author analyzes the characteristics of these families, and seems to conclude that "social isolation" is the main disabling factor in their lives. She relates her findings to the growth of the children in such families, and recommends preventative family services.

50. WOFINDEN, R. C., "Problem Families," Public Health, 57:12 (Sept. 1944), 136-139.
The author discusses a sample of 243 "derelict" families in Rotherham, and briefly describes such a family. The average number of children in such families is high, and in one-fifth of the cases the mother is of low mental standard. The author elaborates on the characteristics and problems found in derelict families, and feels that we should concentrate on the children, in the form of children's homes, and medical education should be re-oriented with accent on the person and home environment and the importance of social factors in disease.

51. --------, "Homeless Children: A Survey of Children in the Scattered Homes, Rotherham," The Medical Officer, 77:19 (May 10, 1947), 185-187.
The author points out that 69.3 per cent of homeless children in Rotherham come from problem families. He urges a nationwide study of problem families including registration of such families. He presents the characteristics of the homeless children; children need special education, and preventative services would have been helpful

in many cases.

52. WOODHOUSE, D. L., "Casework with Problem Families," Case Conf., 5:2 (June 1958), 31-40.
    The author points out the stress caused by social environment on the problem family. The families seem also to be characterized by extreme immaturity. Casework must focus mainly on practical and material assistance. Only limited goals and change must be aimed at in work with these families. The article is illustrated with case material.

53. YOUNGHUSBAND, Eileen L., Report of the Working Party on Social Workers, London: Her Majesty's Stationery Office, 1959, 375 pp.
    This important document on social work in Britain contains at least 25 references to problem families and social work. The index on page 368 will give the reader the various sources of reference to the problem family.

CANADA

54. ALLIN, Kathleen D., "Interim Housing for Troubled Families," Housing Authority of Metropolitan Toronto, Toronto, Ontario, 1959, 5 pp.
    An experiment to construct a two-story, semi-detached house, which would be as nearly "indestructible" as possible and which would be vermin- and fire-proof. This specially constructed house is described in detail (cost $32,000) and was used for a problem family as interim housing. The family which moved in is described, and an evaluation of such housing for problem families is made.

55. AYRES, Beverly, and LAGEY, Joseph C., Checklist Survey of Multi-Problem Families in Vancouver Area, C.C.C. Greater Vancouver Area, 1961, 92 pp.
    The survey identified 1,407 m.p. families in Vancouver in the year of 1960. The report details the characteristics of these families, and includes agency service, and type of problems. A random sample of 100 m.p. families, which proved a representative one, is intensively examined for detailed characteristics. A good case example illustrates the multi-agency contact, and multi-problem guidelines for further research are given. This report is a good example of how a community can begin identifying m.p. families prior to embarking on a project.

56. BECKER, Jane, "The Undeserving Poor," Maclean's, (Nov. 4, 1961), p. 14 ff.
    A popularly written article, giving facts and figures about the m.p. families in Canadian communities. The author discusses the approach to these families in Vancouver, Toronto, London, Charlottetown, Halifax, and Ottawa.

57. BRADLEY, Eleanor, "The Social Service Index - Asset or Liability," (in) <u>Proceedings of the Canadian Conference on Social Work (Vancouver)</u>, Ottawa: Canadian Conference on Social Work, 1950, 214-217.
   The author explores the need for a social service index in order to enable better treatment, diagnosis, and agency co-operation for clients of social agencies.

58. CAMERON, E., CHATTERJEE, P., EDMISON, E., ROBINSON, J., and SHARPE, M., "An Exploratory Study of Two Generation Cases Serviced by Two Children's Aid Societies in Metropolitan Toronto" (unpublished Master's thesis, School of Social Work, University of Toronto, 1962).
   A student group research project under the supervision of Professors Godfrey and Schlesinger. An exploratory study into 50 two-generation families active with two child welfare agencies. The characteristics of these families were found to be similar to those of m.p. families. Each investigator concentrated on a special area in relation to the two-generation family: Housing (Edmison), Illegitimacy (Robinson), Alcoholism (Chatterjee), Disposition of Children (Cameron), Mental Illness (Sharpe). The study thus contains five separate documents.

59. CHEOW, J., GENDRON, P., HORSHAM, B., and VEITCH, B., "The Values of the Multi-Problem Family" (unpublished Master's thesis, School of Social Work, University of Toronto, 1962).
   A group research project under the supervision of Professor John Spencer and Professor Rhinewine. The investigators examined 60 m.p. families in London, Ontario. The objectives included an examination of the characteristics of the sample, agency co-operation, and the value system of the m.p. families. There are four separate documents with different emphasis. Marital Interaction (Cheow), Co-ordination of Services (Gendron), Value System

of the Family (Veitch and Horsham).

60. COMMUNITY CHESTS AND COUNCILS OF THE GREATER VANCOUVER AREA, <u>The Results of a Two-Year Study by the Co-ordination of Services Committee of the Family and Child Welfare Division</u>, C.C.C., Vancouver, British Columbia, 1959, 30 pp.

   This study includes a review of the work done in various communities in North America on m.p. families. Vancouver did an exploratory study of co-ordination of services to 46 m.p. families, and the statistical results are tabulated in the appendix of this report. The committee outlines a proposed area demonstration project, and the objectives and approaches to the project are discussed.

61. ----------, "Proposal for an Area Demonstration Project," C.C.C., Vancouver, British Columbia, 1962, 31 pp. (mimeo.).

   A proposal of a project to work with m.p. families. It includes an appendix which has a synopsis of the joint family services project, a summary of the checklist survey of Vancouver m.p. families, and a summary of treatment approaches to the m.p. family.

62. CONGDON, H. S., "Total Family Treatment instead of Apprehension of Children" (author's unpublished manuscript, Walkerton, Ontario, 1962), 11 pp.

   Paper given as a speech to a Children's Aid Society meeting. The author proposes an approach of "family total treatment" to the chronic family. He relates his approach to the function of the agency, which is the protection of children. Case illustrations are given. He also calculates the costs of removing a child from its own home, or leaving it in the home with family-centred treatment.

63. COOMBE, Dorothy Louise, "Rehabilitation Services for the Chronically Dependent Family" (unpublished Master's thesis, School of Social Work, University of British Columbia, 1961).

    A study of 50 m.p. families, most of whom had been known for 5-10 years by various social agencies in Vancouver. The author reviews the social characteristics, special needs and problems of these families. Studies of other m.p. projects at St. Paul, Vancouver, and London (England) are reviewed. The document attempts to gain enlightenment for an effective approach to chronic dependency.

64. FAMILY SERVICE AGENCY OF GREATER VANCOUVER, "A Caseload Analysis," The Family Service Agency, Vancouver, British Columbia, June 1960, 23 pp. (mimeo.).

    An analysis of the caseload of the above agency covering: characteristics of clientele; range of problems; measurement of improvement; service rendered. Of the sample group selected, comparisons are shown between m.p. families (36 per cent of sample) and non-multi-problem families on the basis of: family composition; occupational classification; income; fee-paying; source of referral. Included in the publication are the Social Service Index Registration for Multi-Problem Families and the check list survey of m.p. families active in caseloads of major agencies as of June 30, 1960.

65. FURNESS, Anne, and WATSON, Ed, "The Implications of the Joint Family Services Project - An Experiment in the Use of Integrated Social Work Methods," C.C.C., Vancouver, British Columbia, 1959, 12 pp. (mimeo.).

    A discussion of a project in Vancouver. The report discusses the implications of the experiment in relation to co-ordination of agencies, casework-group work collaboration, and interprofessional implications in work with m.p. families.

66. JOINT FAMILY SERVICES PROJECT, *An Evaluation of an Experiment in the Use of Integrated Social Work Methods*, C.C.C., Vancouver, British Columbia, 1959, 36 pp.
    A report of the working committee. A co-operative casework-group work approach to work on a "reaching out" basis with families in the community. The experiment covered a 27-months period and involved a family service agency and two local Neighbourhood Houses. The criteria for selection of families are discussed, and the treatment plan is outlined. The appendix contains sections on the work of each agency in the project and a case history illustrates the joint family services approach to m.p. families.

67. KEITH, A. M., "The Chronic Family - Good Money after Bad," *Journal of the Ontario Children's Aid Societies*, 4:8 (Oct. 1961), 1-3.
    A short review of the basic approaches to the m.p. family. Emphasizes co-ordination of agencies, one worker per family, and the costs for projects of working with such families.

68. LAGEY, Joseph, and AYRES, Beverly, *Checklist Survey of Multi-Problem Families in Vancouver City*, C.C.C., Vancouver, British Columbia, 1960, 52 pp. (mimeo.).
    A study to ascertain how many problem families are in Vancouver, where they are located, and what agencies are providing services to them. Fourteen agencies participating in the survey identified 1,684 m.p. families. The characteristics of these families are discussed and illustrated in this report.

69. McEACHERN, W. D. C. (chairman), "Proposal for London Family Centred Project," United Community Services, London, Ontario, 1962, 18 pp. (mimeo.).
    The proposal discusses the background of the F.C.P. project, and the organizations involved in this co-operative attempt to deal

with m.p. families. The report also includes the definition of the m.p. family, and criteria for admission to the project. Five private and public agencies in London will participate in the project of working with 50 m.p. families and 50 other families will remain as a control group.

70. MARCUSE, Berthold, "Long Term Dependency and Maladjustment - Cases in a Family Service Agency" (unpublished Master's thesis, School of Social Work, University of British Columbia, 1956).
    An exploratory study of hard-core cases in a family service setting in Vancouver. A detailed analysis of a small selected group, who manifest all the characteristics of chronic dependency and maladjustment, is included in this investigation.

71. --------, "The Multi-Problem Family - Its Challenge," Soc. Worker, 28:1 (Jan. 1960), 48-57.
    A review of some current studies of the m.p. family, including the study made by the author of "long term" cases at a family agency in Vancouver. Recommendations are made for an approach to m.p. families in their socio-cultural setting.

72. ROBINSON, Marion, "Quiet Revolution," Can. Welf., Part 1, 38:2 (July 1962), 173-175; Part 2, 38:3 (Sept. 1962), 225-227.
    A brief review of the activities of the C.R.A. The author summarizes the St. Paul study, and reviews five principles which have emerged from the programs of prevention and control of psycho-social disorders.

73. ROSEMAN, Renee, "Two hard Core Families" (unpublished Master's thesis, School of Social Work, University of Toronto, 1960).
    An examination of the costs and services of two m.p. families who were active with varied social agencies in Toronto for about 25 years. Their total welfare bill came to

$113,000.

74. SCHLESINGER, Benjamin, "The Problem Family - A Burden on Cities and a Challenge for Social Workers," <u>Globe and Mail</u> (Toronto), Oct. 5, 1961, p. 7.
   A review of the history, definition, and research projects in Canada and the United States on the m.p. family.

75. ――――――, "Multi-Problem Families - A Selected Bibliography," Ontario Welfare Council, Toronto, Ontario, 1961, 7 pp. (mimeo.).
   A specially prepared bibliography, which contains 75 items dealing with m.p. families in Canada, Britain, Holland, and the United States.

76. ――――――, "The Multi-Problem Family: A New Challenge for an Old Problem," <u>Journal of the Ontario Children's Aid Societies</u>, 6:1 (Sept. 1962), 7-8.
   A short review of the work done with m.p. families in five countries around the world, and a request for material for the present annotated bibliography.

77. SCOTT, Barbara, and SPENCER, John, "The Multi-Use Study of Metropolitan Toronto," <u>Social Planning Council</u>, Toronto, Ontario, 1962, 23 pp. (mimeo.).
   A study to look at the duplication of services, collaboration of agencies, and the characteristics of "multi-users". The sample included 1,690 families and individuals, and was drawn from 47 major family-focused health and welfare agencies. The characteristics of the "multi-users" of agencies appear similar to those of m.p. families.

78. THOMSON, Deryck, "Joint Family Services Project, Canada," <u>Can. Welf.</u>, 34:1 (May 1958), 14-19.
   A description of a project in Vancouver to try to develop more effective methods for preventive work with families. The project

included 170 families. The teamwork approach of agencies resulted in positive changes in these families.

79. UNITED COMMUNITY SERVICES, "Multi-Problem Family Project," United Community Services, London, Ontario, 1961, 3 pp. (mimeo.).
    A summary of the activities leading up to the formation of a committee to organize the Multi-Problem Family Project in London.

80. ----------, "Report of the Research Committee on Multi-Problem Families," United Community Services, London, Ontario, 1961, 4 pp. (mimeo.).
    Report of the committee, who reviewed projects active in England and the United States, and made recommendations as to the approach in London.

81. WEISS, David, "Multi-Problem Families - How Can Community Services Be Mobilized for More Effective Services to Them," Canadian Welfare Council, Ottawa, Ontario, Jan. 1960, 4 pp. (mimeo.).
    A condensed version of a speech discussing the motivations and capacity of the m.p. family, as well as the opportunities available to them. A plea is made for mobilizing community services for such families.

82. WELFARE COUNCIL OF GREATER WINDSOR, "Definition and Operational Definition of Terms of Multi-Problem Family as used in Windsor, Ontario," Welfare Council, Windsor, Ontario, 1961, 4 pp. (mimeo.).
    This memo discusses the terms used in defining an m.p. family.

83. WELFARE COUNCIL OF OTTAWA, Multi-Problem Families, Welfare Council, Ottawa, Ontario, 1961, 39 pp.
    A survey of 47 m.p. families known to health and welfare agencies in Ottawa. The findings include the characteristics of these families, and discuss the use of community

resources. The appendix includes the survey questionnaire and a summary of statistical findings.

84. ---------, "Draft Statement to Offer Special Services to Multi-Problem Families," Welfare Council, Ottawa, Ontario, 1962, 5 pp. (mimeo.).

A proposal for a project to work with 50-60 m.p. families in Ottawa. The objectives are outlined, and the need for small caseloads in such a project are spelled out. Costs are calculated.

FRANCE

85. BUREAU DE RECHERCHES SOCIALES, "Groupe d'Étude sur les Familles Inadaptées," Aide à Toute Détresse, Paris, 1962, 4 pp. (mimeo.).
    An outline of a proposed course of study to be given by our French and Belgian colleagues on the m.p. family (famille inadaptée), to include sociological and psychological factors. The detailed outline indicates an intensive approach to the study of this problem. The organizing group is planning a series of monographs in 1962-63, for use as a basis for study.

86. WRESINSKI, l'Abbé Joseph, "Notes sur la famille inadaptée dans la Societé moderne," Aide à Toute Détresse, Paris, 1962, 20 pp. (mimeo.).
    The French-Belgian terminology for the m.p. family is "la famille inadaptée". In this paper the author uses the term "familles sous-privilégiées", a translation of the use of "underprivileged families" in use in England. The author includes origin of the m.p. family, the psychology of the family, and possibilities of rehabilitation. The second part of the paper is devoted to remedies, and includes approaches to the family through re-education, casework, team approach and environmental changes, and a centre similar to the Dutch Zuidplein project.

(See also annotations under "Miscellaneous" which arrived too late to be included here.)

HOLLAND

87. BURGESS, Irene L., "Homeless Families in the Netherlands," <u>Case Conf.</u>, 1:7 (Nov. 1954), 20-22.

    A report and description of the "controlled" housing unit projects at Utrecht and Rotterdam, Holland. The units house non-voluntary, anti-social, problem and evicted families. The aim of the projects is, on a long-term basis, to re-educate and rehabilitate the families for life in ordinary communities. Treatment method involves the use of casework, educational work, and recreational facilities and skills. A family unit is kept together, unless, after long-term casework, it is diagnosed as a "sick biological unit".

88. HOBMAN, Daisy L., "Re-Education Centres for Problem Families in Holland," <u>Quart. Rev.</u>, 291:595 (Jan. 1953), 62-71.

    Problem families are classified into three categories: weak or unstable, asocial, and anti-social. They are referred to the ten centres, each containing 10-20 families, and remain there for 3-5 years. The author describes fully the work and life at one of these Re-Education Centres for Problem Families.

89. MILL, J. van, <u>The Zuidplein Project</u>, Municipal Welfare Department, Rotterdam, 1953, 16 pp.

    A description of the Rotterdam experiment for the rehabilitation of socially weak families. Families all over Holland who need re-education are referred to this project. The family is then trained in housekeeping, budgetting, child welfare, and other family responsibilities. A map of the project site is included.

90. MINISTRY FOR SOCIAL WORK, <u>Problems of Socially Maladjusted Families in the Netherlands</u>, Ministry for Social Work, The Hague, 1958, 15 pp.

A short history of the projects for m.p. families in Holland from 1923 to 1958. It discusses the centres of re-education, which were established after World War II. The "Zuidplein" and "Ravelin" projects are briefly surveyed.

91. --------, *Sociale Integratie Problee mgezinner*, The Hague: Staats drukkerij - Uitgevers bedritjf, 1960.
    Complete report of the committee to fight against social maladjustment. An excerpt can be found in annotation #93.

92. --------, *Problem Families in The Netherlands*, Ministry for Social Work, The Hague, 1960, 8 pp.
    A definition for the Dutch problem family is given and discussed, and the main characteristics of the "socially maladjusted" family are enumerated. The survey covered 2,501 households. The second half of this pamphlet deals with the approach to the problem family in Holland, and briefly mentions the types of treatment offered to them.

93. --------, *Report on the Social Integration of Problem Families*, Ministry for Social Work, The Hague, 1961, 9 pp.
    Excerpt of a report of a committee to advise on matters relating to the fight against social maladjustment. It briefly discusses the integration of problem families and society, housing, and the concentration of problem families. The task of social work is then set forth in the re-education work with problem families.

94. QUERIDO, A., "Problem Family in the Netherlands," *The Medical Officer*, 75:20 (May 18, 1946), 193-195.
    A description of the "Zeeburgerdorp" (village) for problem families, a small street of 52 one-storied homes, each containing 3 or 4 rooms. The families living in this district could be divided into three groups:

(1) conditional-social (once some conditions of health worked out, family can return to community); (2) conditional-unsocial (without outside help this family will founder); and (3) unconditional-unsocial (social assistance is powerless to prevent their deterioration). The author goes on to discuss this type of village program for problem families.

95. SHERIDAN, Mary D., "The Rehabilitation of Unsatisfactory Families in the Netherlands," Public Health, 69:3 (Dec. 1955), 62-64.

    A complete review of the Zuidplein project at Rotterdam. The author discusses the housing estate for m.p. families, and relates the administrative and residential program of this unique project. A map illustrates the layout of the housing estate for m.p. families.

96. --------, "The Rehabilitation of Unsatisfactory Families in the Netherlands," Public Health, 69:4 (Jan. 1956), 80-83.

    A further exposition of the Zuidplein project with special emphasis on social work, re-education, financing, and admission procedures. The future of the centre is discussed.

97. SPURGIN, Clare, "Problem Families in Holland," The Magistrate, 9:18 (Nov.-Dec. 1952), 251-252.

    Description of a visit to "Ten Arlo" centre at Zuidwolde in the north of Holland. The author discusses the program of the project for problem families in relation to admission, living conditions, and re-education program.

UNITED STATES

98. ALAMEDA COUNTY WELFARE DEPARTMENT, <u>Aid to Needy Children - Intensive Services Unit Research Project</u>, Council on Social Planning, Alameda County, Oakland, California, 1962, 56 pp.
    A project of intensive casework services for 18 months to families receiving Aid to Needy Children. Four social workers carried caseloads of 35 instead of the usual 100. The project had a control group, equal to the special project group (115 cases in each group). About 70 per cent of the families were Negro. The report discusses in detail the characteristics of the families and the type of service offered. The project emphasized "safeguarding of children". The appendix contains 30 statistical tables which give complete detail about the characteristics of the groups. Intensive casework helped the families in relation to their children and themselves.

99. ALLEGHENY COUNTY BOARD OF ASSISTANCE, <u>The Rehabilitation Demonstration</u>, Department of Public Welfare, Pittsburgh, Pennsylvania, Apr. 1959, 31 pp.
    A 5-year demonstration project of the rehabilitation potentials of public assistant recipients (1953-1958). Cases (200) with a long history of dependency were selected at random, and 4 caseworkers, a clerk, and supervisor composed the unit staff. The caseload was later reduced to 35. The report discusses the characteristics of the cases, the type and amount of service given, and case illustrations are noted to show the work of the unit. An analysis of the work of the unit is statistically presented.

100. AUSTIN, David, "The Special Youth Program Approach to Chronic Problem Families," (in) <u>Community Organization 1958</u>, New York: Columbia University Press, 1958, 101-108.

Discussion of the Special Youth Program of the Greater Boston Council for Youth, a project of work with adolescents of "chronic families" who were identified through the Social Service Exchange. Five agencies co-operated in a co-ordinated project, and the plan of action is outlined by the author.

101. AYRES, Beverly, <u>Economic Dependencies in F.C.P. Families: Can It Be Reduced?</u>, C.C.C., St. Paul, Minnesota, 1961, 66 pp.

Description of the economic situation of 150 F.C.P. families, including a historical review of the economic pattern of these families, illustrated with statistical tables. A case history of economic rehabilitation in one m.p. family is given. The final part includes a detailed review of the Public Assistance costs for all F.C.P. families.

102. BADEN STREET SETTLEMENT, <u>Volunteer Case Aide Demonstration Project</u>, Baden Street Settlement, Rochester, New York, 1959, 75 pp.

This book describes the Volunteer Case Aide Project (V.C.A.), financed by the Junior League, and summarizes the selection of families, case aides, and approaches in this novel project. Results and findings are given, and an evaluation of the project is made. A lengthy appendix includes record forms, family summaries, and letters of appreciation from various community sources.

103. ----------, <u>Patterns of Change in Families Assigned to the Volunteer Case Aide Program</u>, Baden Street Settlement, Rochester, New York, 1960, 24 pp. (mimeo.).

Review of the characteristics of the 42 m.p. families in the V.C.A. program. A summary of 12 family histories is included in the material.

104. ――――――, *Reaching Out to Hard-to-Reach, Multi-Problem Families through the Use of Volunteer Case Aides*, Baden Street Settlement, Rochester, New York, 1961, 11 pp. (mimeo.).

   Discussion of nine closed cases in the V.C.A. project. The paper includes a financial statement which indicates the cost of the program. Recommendations are made for further study and work.

105. ――――――, *Volunteer Case Aide Services to Families with Problems*, Baden Street Settlement, Rochester, New York, 1962, 12 pp. (mimeo.).

   This paper discusses the activities of the volunteers in relation to service to the 42 families in the V.C.A. project. Case examples illustrate this novel approach.

106. BAKER, Mary S., *Memorandum on Implications for Social Work Curriculum of Community Research Associates' Materials*, C.S.W.E., New York City, Mar. 1960, 23 pp.

   Review of the major concepts and methodology used in the various research studies conducted by the Community Research Associates, Inc. These materials are assessed in the context of their relevance and significance for curriculum content in schools of social work. Use in specific courses is examined and methods of introduction into the curriculum are briefly discussed. A bibliography of the materials reviewed is appended.

107. BARBOUR, Harold S., BAUGHN, Benjamin, FISHER, Grace, and HARRIS, William, "An Experiment in Intensive Special Case Handling of Multi-Problem Families," School District of Philadelphia, Pennsylvania, 1961, Report #1, 8 pp.

   Report of a pilot project of 37 cases of children of m.p. families who came to the attention of the Attendance Department. Involved in these cases were 123 children of school age and 48 pre-school children. The report discusses the selection and approach in working with these families.

108. ———————, "An Experiment in Intensive Special Case Handling of Multi-Problem Families," School District of Philadelphia, Pennsylvania, 1961, Report #2, 21 pp.
    This report looks back at the experiment after one year of service. Case records illustrate the approach and effect of the m.p. family project. The report also summarizes the characteristics found in the m.p. families and their children. The project is continuing.

109. BEHRENS, Marjorie L., and ACKERMAN, Nathan W., "The Home Visit as an Aid in Family Diagnosis and Therapy," Soc. Casewk., 37:1 (Jan. 1956), 11-19.
    Description of the use of the home visit as an aid in family diagnosis and therapy where the original patient is a child. The article contains numerous practical suggestions for use in the diagnosis of the needs of an m.p. family.

110. BEISSER, Paul T., and VAN VLEET, Phyllis P., Early Identification of Behavior Problem Children and Multi-Problem Families, Superintendent of Schools, San Mateo County, California, 1962, 81 pp.
    The authors developed a behaviour rating scale with which a classroom teacher can identify a significant proportion of young children whose school behaviour indicates families with problems resulting in overt behaviour disorder or financial dependency or both. The authors used a sophisticated research design which included controlled and experimental groups of school children. The study includes statistical data to show the usefulness of the behavioural scale in identifying m.p. families through their children. The appendix includes the scale used, and a family classification and case management schedule.

111. BEMMELS, Violet G., "Seven Fighting Families," <u>Soc. Wk.</u>, 5:1 (Jan. 1960), 91-99.

    A project in New York City, which involved 7 families characterized by anti-social and hostile behaviour. The majority of the children were delinquents. One social worker handled the co-ordination of community resources for each family and treatment procedures are described. Improvement was indicated in the behaviour of the families after 2 years. A tentative evaluation of their responsiveness is offered by the author.

112. BENDER, Ann, "Clarifying the Service to Families with Many Problems - The Family Agency," <u>J. Soc. Wk. Process</u>, 11 (1960), 90-92.

    Discussion of Rappaport's paper (240). The author, who is on the staff of the Family Service of Northern Delaware, discusses the m.p. family in relation to service offered by the agency.

113. BERG, Maybelle F., "Challenge of the Difficult Family," <u>Pub. Welf.</u>, 15:3 (July 1957), 107-111.

    Discussion of the recognition of early signs of breakdown in m.p. families. The author points out the attitudes and approaches which a social worker must have in order to prevent or alleviate such situations. A case illustration is included.

114. BIRT, Charles J., <u>The Significance of the Family Unit Report Study to Community Planning</u>, C.C.C., St. Paul, Minnesota, 1950, 11 pp. (mimeo.).

    Summary of the findings of the 1948 Family Unit Report Study. The facts indicate that 6 per cent of the families in St. Paul required 68 per cent of the dependency services, 55 per cent of the adjustment services, and 46 per cent of the health services. The welfare costs were 5.5 million dollars.

115. --------, "Family Centered Project of St. Paul," Soc. Wk., 1:6 (Oct. 1956), 41-47.
    An early discussion of the F.C.P., outlining joint agency co-operation. The author also discusses the most serious types of problem related to families of the F.C.P.

116. BISHOP, Ann Julia, "Clarifying the Service to Families with Many Problems - The Protective Agency," J. Soc. Wk. Process, 11 (1960), 88-89.
    Discussion of Rappaport's paper (#240), in relation to a 3-year project of intensive work with m.p. families of the Pennsylvania Society to Protect Children from Cruelty.

117. BRADSHAW, Dawson, "What One Community Is Doing about Multi-Problem Families," Family Service Highlights, 18:9 (Nov. 1957), 129-133.
    Brief review of the planning and accomplishments of the F.C.P. project in St. Paul.

118. BRICKMAN, Leonard, "Finding Leadership in a Low-Income Urban Area," Adult Leadership, 9:9 (Mar. 1961), 273-274.
    Discussion of leadership training in East Harlem, New York. The author outlines the course given to leaders in this low-income area.

119. BROWNE, Ann, Multi-Problem Families, Council of Social Planning, Berkeley, California, 1961, 22 pp.
    Report of the Berkeley Project of 47 m.p. families. Statistical data illustrate the characteristics of these families, and the problems presented are documented and discussed. Case illustrations are given.

120. --------, Multi-Problem Families - Phase II, Council of Social Planning, Berkeley, California, 1962, 8 pp.
    Second report of a study of 47 Berkeley m.p. families covering the community resources available, the uses made of these resources,

and the need to extend additional services. Case histories are discussed in relation to the above areas of concern.

121. BRUBAKER, Susan, "Possibilities of Prevention of Damage to Children in Multi-Problem Families," (author's unpublished manuscript, Philadelphia, Pennsylvania, 1962, 12 pp.).
The author presents evidence and develops the thesis that the primary causative factor of the mental disturbances most prevalent in m.p. families is the very inadequate and inconsistent parenting to which the children are exposed. These mental disturbances, the patterns of which are passed on from parents to children, fall predominantly into two classifications: schizophrenia and character disorders. The author stresses the point that preventative programs should begin "at least in pre-natal and post-natal stages". She points out that these families should be easily identifiable and the need for services predicted.

122. BRYANT, Clara Bay, "Clarifying the Service to Families with Many Problems - The School," J. Soc. Wk. Process, 11 (1960), 93-96.
Discussion of Rappaport's paper (#240). The author, who is associated with the Division of Pupil Personnel and Counseling in Philadelphia, relates a case situation of a school-age child belonging to an m.p. family.

123. BUCK, Carl, BUELL, Bradley, and KANDLE, R. P., "Family Health in Tomorrow's Community," Amer. J. Pub. Health, 41:10 (Oct. 1951), 1258-1262.
Discussion of the health services used by the families in the St. Paul F.C.P. The startling finding emerged that 6 per cent of the families studied in 1948 absorbed 40 per cent of organized health services, 55 per cent of adjustment services (correctional, mental health) and 68 per cent of the dependency services. Health problems were interrelated with other family problems.

124. BUELL, Bradley, "Know What the What Is," <u>Survey Midmonthly</u> Oct. 1948, 4 pp. (reprint available from C.R.A.).
Discusses the reasons why St. Paul, Minnesota, was chosen as a community to test out survey technique of C.R.A. The method was called the "Family Unit Report System". An early article which gives some insight into the planning of the F.C.P. of St. Paul.

125. --------, "Preventing and Controlling Disordered Behavior," <u>Mental Hygiene</u>, 39:3 (July 1955), 365-375.
Discussion of three elements of a preventive program, as used by the C.R.A. in three projects in Winona (Minnesota), Washington County (Maryland), and San Mateo (California).

126. --------, "Retooling for Prevention," C.R.A., New York City, 1956, 19 pp. (mimeo.).
The author describes five research and experimental projects in the U.S.A. and discusses the procedures used. It appears that dependency, indigent disability, and disordered behaviour account for about three-fourths of community caseloads.

127. --------, "Retooling for Human Betterment," C.R.A., New York City, 1956, 15 pp. (mimeo.).
Discussion of how the four basic human problems of dependency, ill-health, maladjustment, and recreational needs tend to cluster in the same family groups. These findings are related to the St. Paul F.C.P. study. The author points out the need for a systematic plan for the prevention and reduction of the problems creating the need for community services.

128. --------, <u>Is Prevention Possible?</u> C.R.A., New York City, 1959, 20 pp.
Address given as the Eduard C. Lindeman Memorial Lecture in San Francisco, California. The author discusses the evidence which supports.

the need for prevention, in relation to various C.R.A. projects. He outlines briefly the findings of these projects and discusses future goals in preventative work.

129. BUELL, Bradley, and ASSOCIATES, <u>Community Planning for Human Services</u>, New York: Columbia University Press, 1952, 464 pp.
    The book is based on research done by C.R.A. The report presents material in the four areas of need: dependency, ill-health, maladjustment, and recreation. For each of these areas the authors discuss descriptive material on the nature of the problem, the basic services needed in the community, and the type of structures set up to provide these services. The material is also based to a certain degree on the St. Paul F.C.P.

130. BUELL, Bradley, BEISSER, Paul T., and WEDEMEYER, John M., "Reorganizing to Prevent and Control Disordered Behavior," <u>Mental Hygiene</u>, 42:2 (Apr. 1958), 155-194.
    Report of an experiment in community planning and organization in San Mateo County, California, in 1954 by the C.R.A. Intensive family diagnosis is stressed in planning for 231 m.p. families in the area. The characteristics of families with disordered behaviour are discussed, and the authors develop four distinctive types of families. Types of treatment are recommended and discussed.

131. BURGESS, Ernest W., "Economic, Cultural, and Social Factors in Family Breakdown," <u>Amer. J. Orthopsychiat.</u>, 24:3 (July 1954), 462-470.
    Part 1 of this paper presents an analysis of factors in family breakdown in terms of the prevailing cultural values of individualism, competition, and democracy. In Part 2, the author deals with prevention of family breakdown and rehabilitation.

132. CASE CONFERENCE, "Case Conference on a Multi-Problem Family," <u>Children</u>, 8:3 (May-June 1961), 106-110.

A case conference on a m.p. family who had "fallen through" the network of agency services, with no single agency taking responsibility for "seeing the family through" over a long period of time. The paper includes a case history and commentaries by a public health nurse, a medical educator, a public health pediatrician, and a public welfare worker.

133. CHAREN, Sol, LIEBENBERG, Beatrice, SHERESHEF-SKY, Pauline M., and WARD, Henry P., "The Use of the Family Approach in Working with Children in Seriously Disturbed Families," J. Amer. Academy of Child Psychiat., 1:3 (July 1962), 462-476.

    Discussion of therapeutic work with the m.p. family in the Child Guidance Clinic of the Jewish Social Service Agency in Washington, D.C. Case illustrations help to point up the importance of the therapeutic impact of the therapist's faith in the family. This family-centred orientation, in a Child Guidance Clinic, seems to bring about a modest success in the use of psychotherapy for the m.p. family.

134. CHEMUNG COUNTY, "Research Demonstration Project with Dependent Multi-Problem Families," Chemung County, Elmira, New York, 1962 (two papers, 4 pp. and 7 pp.).

    Two short statistical reports (Feb. 1, 1962, Sept. 1962), on the sampling methods used in the project. For the sampling pool, which consisted of experimental and control groups, 195 cases of m.p. families were drawn. Of this group 50 families will be served by two caseworkers on an intensive basis. The papers give statistical data of the composition of the sample pool.

135. CHRISTENSEN, Harold (ed.), Families under Stress - Handbook of Marriage and the Family, New York: Rand McNally (to be published in 1963).

    In this book Donald Hansen and Reuben Hill will have a chapter on "Families under

Stress", which discusses m.p. families.

136. CLARK, Irving, Report to Supporting Foundations - Family Centered Project, C.C.C., St. Paul, Minnesota, 1961, 35 pp.
    Reviews the project operations during 1948-1959, and includ s future proposals for 1959-1963. A progress report is made for 1960-61, which includes future goals. The appendix includes a profile of the F.C.P. 1948-1963, and a complete bibliography of F.C.P. materials.

137. COHEN, Wilbur, and BERNARD, Sydney E., The Prevention and Reduction of Dependency, Washtenaw County Department of Social Welfare, Ann Arbor, Michigan, 1961, 94 pp.
    This booklet discusses the special services project of Washtenaw County, which attempted to demonstrate the effects of introducing social work skills into an existing public welfare program. The project included 30 m.p. families, comprising 159 individuals. Case illustrations are given, detailed steps of the approach are outlined, and recommendations are made for further research.

138. COLORADO STATE DEPARTMENT OF WELFARE, "Public Assistance Services to Multi-Problem Families," The Library Counselor, 14:3 (July 1959), 22 pp. (mimeo.).
    An annotated bibliography of m.p. families and Public Assistance, compiled by Mrs. Davidson, the Librarian of the Colorado Department of Public Welfare. It is a thorough annotation and includes books, pamphlets, projects, and articles, all of the United States.

139. COMMUNITY COUNCIL OF THE ATLANTA AREA, "Neighborhood Program," C.C., Atlanta, Georgia, 1961, 10 pp. (mimeo.).
    A proposal for a 5-year program of intensive family casework with m.p. families. A complete budget is outlined for the project, and the list of 12 participating agencies is included.

140. ————, *Atlanta and the Multi-Problem Family*, C.C., Atlanta, Georgia, 1962, 35 pp.

　　An analysis of 48 m.p. families. The report contains statistical details of the characteristics of these families. The findings include the facts that m.p. families are larger, have more children, more broken families, and are more dependent on social services than other Atlanta families. The multiplicity of problems, preventive and rehabilitative potentialities are enumerated. Case summaries illustrate the type of m.p. family found in Atlanta.

141. COMMUNITY COUNCIL OF GREATER NEW YORK, *Ways of Strengthening Family Life*, C.C., New York City, Feb. 6, 1958, 53 pp.

　　Proceedings of the Community Council of Greater New York Conference on Preventative Services. Among other topics covered in this report are co-operative planning to strengthen the breaking family, and counselling to m.p. families as a public responsibility.

142. COMMUNITY RESEARCH ASSOCIATES, *C.R.A.*, C.R.A., New York City (no date), 10 pp.

　　Pamphlet outlining the work of C.R.A. and the research and surveys carried out by this organization.

143. ————, *The Prevention and Control of Indigent Disability in Washington County, Maryland*, C.R.A., New York City, 1954, 119 pp.

　　A study of 1,317 m.p. families, who constitute 5.9 per cent of the total number of families in Washington County. The characteristics and problems of these families are documented and suggestions for treatment are made. The appendix contains 21 statistical tables, of which three compare four C.R.A. studies of San Mateo, Winona, Ramsey, and Washington County. Other tables detail characteristics of the m.p. families in Washington County only.

144. COMMUNITY SERVICES CENTER, <u>First Evaluation of the Community Services Center</u>, United South End Settlements, Boston, Massachusetts, 1961, 30 pp.
 A report about the casework-group work-community organization activities of the Center, which is located in the South End Housing Project in Boston, containing 1,850 people, in a 60:40 per cent Negro-White ratio. Forty per cent of the families are on public assistance. The report reviews the problems presented by the tenants, and discusses the special problems of 213 families who needed casework service. The group work and community organization aspects of the Center are reviewed, and statistics are given for inter-agency co-operation on the families in the project. The conclusions include the facts that teamwork is effective, reaching-out to families gets good results, and locating the Center within the housing project facilitates service.

145. COMMUNITY WELFARE COUNCIL OF GREATER MILWAUKEE, "Suggested Project Plan for Improving Social Services," C.W.C., Milwaukee, Wisconsin, Feb. 23, 1960, 14 pp. (mimeo.).
 This publication includes the following: (1) Suggested Project Plan for Improving Social Services, Oct. 21, 1958; (2) a digest of the above, Feb. 23, 1960; and (3) Revised Project Plan for Improving Social Services, Sept. 16, 1959.

146. COMPTON, Beulah R., "The Family Centered Project and Correction," C.C.C., St. Paul, Minnesota, 1959, 16 pp. (mimeo.).
 Discussion of the social characteristics of the m.p. families in the F.C.P., including family structure, health statistics, and agencies involved in service. Figures are given as to the successful outcome of the F.C.P. The author also explores the motivations and needs of the m.p. families.

147. ----------, "The Story of the Family Centered Project," C.C.C., St. Paul, Minnesota, 1961, 7 pp. (mimeo.).

   A good summary of the F.C.P. from its beginnings in 1948, when the first study was carried out by C.R.A. Casework operations began in 1954, with help from the Hill Foundation. Methods and approaches to the m.p. families are discussed.

148. CONLAN, Mildred, "Screening Report," C.C.C., St. Paul, Minnesota, 1954, 14 pp. (mimeo.).

   Report on case reading of m.p. family situations. The author discusses treatment in relation to father, mother, and children. Strengths of the families are also explored. The article is illustrated with case material.

149. COUNCIL ON SOCIAL WORK EDUCATION, Concepts of Prevention and Control: Their Use in the Social Work Curriculum, C.S.W.E., New York City, 1961, 32 pp.

   Report of a workshop to discuss the use of C.R.A. and F.C.P. St. Paul material in schools of social work.

150. CRAWFORD, Fred R., The Forgotten Egg, Department of Health, Division of Mental Health, Austin, Texas, 1961, 43 pp.

   A study of m.p. families of Mexican-American descent in the neighbourhood of the Good Samaritan Center in San Antonio, Texas. The author discusses the social characteristics of the families in the neighbourhood, which contains 3,156 family units. Twenty-four cases were selected for special study, since the children were having difficulties in first grade. The family relationships of the children are briefly reviewed, and considerations for service are outlined by the investigator. The appendix contains case illustrations.

151. DICK, K., and STRNAD, L., "The Multi-Problem Family and Problems of Service," Soc. Casewk., 39:6 (June 1958), 349-355.

   The m.p. families appear to have little

to give to their children, and thus dependency and service are perpetuated to the next generation. The lack of success of working with this type of family is discussed, and communication is recognized as one of the barriers to reaching them.

152. DOUGLAS COUNTY WELFARE ADMINISTRATION, <u>Family Rehabilitation Program</u>, Douglas County Welfare Administration, Omaha, Nebraska, Mar. 1962, 52 pp.

   Report of the new program for family rehabilitation operating in Douglas County under the Assistance Bureau. The program is directed toward the economic, physical, social, and emotional rehabilitation of families receiving assistance under the public welfare programs. The approach can be described as "problem-solving" and "family-unit centred". C.R.A. methods are used to identify the m.p. families. All families are classified in terms of pathology, and are dealt with accordingly within a "three levels of service" treatment plan. The need for a team approach is noted.

153. ELLER, Glowe C., HATCHER, Gordon H., and BUELL, Bradley, "Health and Welfare Issues in Community Planning for the Problem of Indigent Disability," <u>Amer. J. Pub. Health</u>, 48:11 (Nov. 1958), 1-49.

   Report of a project in Washington County, Maryland, using an interdisciplinary treatment approach with 400 families, based on family diagnosis. Operational methods consisted of a family reporting system and a diagnostic work-up and treatment plan. The treatment plan, methods of prognosis, rehabilitative goals, and treatment results are described.

154. ERIE WELFARE COUNCIL, "Welfare Council Multi-Problem Family Project, 1959," Welfare Council, Erie, Pennsylvania, 8 pp. (mimeo.).

   A report on the m.p. family project in Erie County. The primary aim of the project is "to prevent and reduce community-wide problems" through more effective and efficient health, welfare, and recreation services.

155. FAMILY SERVICE ASSOCIATION OF INDIANAPOLIS, A Three-Year Demonstration in the Rehabilitation of Sixteen Families, F.S.A., Indianapolis, Indiana, 1961, 38 pp.
    The characteristics of 16 m.p. families selected for the project are given, the methods of help described, and the results evaluated. The latter seem to have been quite successful in terms of social work goals and community expectations. Financial expenditures on behalf of the families were reduced, owing to the efforts of the intensive approach. A full case illustration is given in the appendix.

156. FANTL, Berta, "Integrating Psychological, Social, and Cultural Factors in Assertive Casework," Soc. Wk., 3:4 (Oct. 1958), 30-37.
    A psychologically oriented article in which the author urges that psychological, social, and cultural factors be integrated in the use of assertive casework with "hard to reach" families. She analyzes the personality of the "hard to reach" client and examines the influence of socio-cultural factors on him.

157. ---------, "Casework in Lower Class Districts," Mental Hygiene, 45:3 (July 1961), 425-438.
    A plea to consider not only the child-parent relationships, but also the community's perception of the clients. The author writes from experience in attempting to do casework with m.p. families in a highly crowded, poor, and delinquent area in San Francisco. She feels that we have to put the "social" back into social work and see the environment in a new dynamic way.

158. ————, "Preventive Intervention," Soc. Wk., 7:3 (July 1962), 41-47.
A description of a small project, where a social work agency related to school guidance moved into a lower lower-class district. The author illustrates the article with a case history to show how possible lines of intervention on behalf of the client by the social worker can be helpful in problem families.

159. FIKE, Norma, "Social Treatment of Long-Term Dependency," Soc. Wk., 2:4 (Oct. 1957), 51-57.
The author discusses families who are incapable of independent functioning for more than brief periods. She writes from a medical setting, and illustrates chronic maladjustment by a lengthy case history. She advocates preventive casework for many such dependent families.

160. FISHER, Seymour, and MENDELL, Daniel, "The Communication of Neurotic Patterns over Two and Three Generations," J. for Study of Interp. Processes, 19:1 (Feb. 1956), 41-46.
An attempt to document the extent of similarity of conflict of behaviour from one generation to another in families. Repetition patterns of neurotic behaviour were apparent in this generational study. Of interest to workers with m.p. families.

161. ————, "An Approach to Neurotic Behavior in Terms of a Three Generation Family Model," J. of Nervous and Mental Disease, 123:2 (Feb. 1956), 171-180.
A study involving 14 families of two generations of kin and six families of three generations of kin. By using case material the authors illustrate a conceptual approach in understanding the individual patient as one link in an on-going generational group process.

162. --------, "A Multi-Generation Approach to
        Treatment of Psychopathology," *J. of Nervous and Mental Disease*, 126:6 (June 1958),
        523-529.
    Information obtained by the authors,
through test material, about two and three
generational neurotic behaviour patterns in
families was used to determine prognosis of
therapeutic treatment for individuals in the
generational families. Case illustrations
are used to demonstrate this approach to
family therapy.

163. FOSSIER, Mildred, "Some Aspects of Work with
        Children in Their Own Homes: A Special
        Look at the "Hard to Reach" Family," Department of Public Welfare, New Orleans,
        Louisiana, 1960, 10 pp. (mimeo.).
    Paper given at a regional American Public
Welfare meeting, which discusses the social
worker-client relationship in work with the
hard-to-reach family. It traces the feelings
of the caseworker, who despite large caseloads attempts to deal with the needs of problem families.

164. GEISMAR, Ludwig L., "The Family Centered
        Project of St. Paul," C.C.C., St. Paul,
        Minnesota, 1957, 15 pp. (mimeo.).
    Report to the Research Section of the
Kansas Conference of Social Work. Includes
a brief history, the setting, description of
the project families, the community organization aspect of the project and the research
methods used in the St. Paul classic study
of m.p. families.

165. --------, "Social Functioning of the Multi-
        Problem Family," *Mental Hygiene*, 43:2
        (Apr. 1959), 290-295.
    Role performance and levels of social
functioning are measured in m.p. families of
the St. Paul F.C.P. It is suggested that
such data as indices of family disorganization may be developed.

166. ────────, "The Multi-Problem Family: Significance of Research Findings," (in) <u>Social Welfare Forum 1960</u>, New York: Columbia University Press, 1960, 166-179.
    Summary of some of the most important findings of the St. Paul F.C.P. The patterns of the m.p. family are reviewed, and malfunctioning of the family is examined. The author develops a hypothesis for the study of the process of disorganization in m.p. families.

167. ────────, "Three levels of Treatment for the Multi-Problem Family," <u>Soc. Casewk.</u>, 42:3 (Mar. 1961), 124-127.
    Report of the project carried out by the New Haven, Connecticut, Public Housing Authorities. The three levels of services offered to m.p. families were family-centred treatment, neighbourhood groups, and professional intervention through community channels.

168. ────────, "Applying an Operational Definition of Family Function in Determining Need for Services" (author's unpublished paper, New Brunswick, New Jersey, 1962, 13 pp.).
    Paper presented at a meeting of the American Sociological Association attempts to explain a method of objective assessment of need for services as a basic element in community welfare planning. The author presents an outline for a standardized Evaluation of Family Functioning. He discusses his sampling method using 320 families from five agencies, among whom 150 were m.p. families in Minnesota.

169. GEISMAR, Ludwig L., and AYRES, Beverly, <u>Families in Trouble</u>, C.C.C., St. Paul, Minnesota, 1958, 142 pp.
    A study of common social characteristics of 100 m.p. families. Generation-to-generation pattern of use of agencies was evident in this study. F.C.P. families were characterized by inability to function in accordance with community standards in most fields of social functioning.

170. ————, Patterns of Change in Problem Families, C.C.C., St. Paul, Minnesota, 1959, 48 pp.
    Detailed description of the areas of family functioning according to frequency of problem in 150 families in the F.C.P. in St. Paul. The authors describe treatment approaches by the social workers, and briefly review a study of 30 families who had been subjected to family-centred casework. The appendix charts the levels of social functioning in m.p. families.

171. ————, "A Method for Evaluating the Social Functioning of Families under Treatment," Soc. Wk., 4:1 (Jan. 1959), 102-109.
    Description of how family functioning was measured in the St. Paul F.C.P. The three main levels of functioning were: inadequate functioning, marginal functioning, and adequate functioning. Thirty-six families were studied on the basis of this scale of functioning.

172. ————, Measuring Family Functioning, C.C.C., St. Paul, Minnesota, 1960, 124 pp.
    A manual for evaluating the social functioning of disorganized families. The appendix contains a lengthy outline for social diagnosis and yearly evaluations of families in the F.C.P. in St. Paul. Levels of social functioning are also detailed in the appendix. Of value to communities who are planning to institute projects on the m.p. family, because of the picture it presents of the complicated and intense methods required to measure family functioning.

173. GEISMAR, Ludwig L., and LA SORTE, Michael A., The Multi-Problem Family (to be published in 1963).
    This book will include conceptual clarification of the m.p. family terminology, and problems of identification and measurement. The authors will also report on a study of 70 low-income families.

174. GEISMAR, L. L., LA SORTE, M. A., and AYRES, B., "Measuring Family Disorganization," Marr. Fam. Living, 24:1 (Feb. 1962), 51-56.
   Description of a technique for measuring family functioning by means of rating role performance of family members in nine categories of social functioning, as developed in the St. Paul project of m.p. families. The number of m.p. families studied was 150, and results show that this type of family has greatest difficulty with interpersonal relationships within the family.

175. GIDEON, Henry J., and BARGANS, Richard, Agencies Cooperate to Help the Troubled Family, National Federation of Settlements and Neighborhood Centers, New York City, 1958, 9 pp.
   Report of a Case Conference approach used in the Germantown Settlement in Philadelphia. Case illustration is also used in this article. Eight agencies from the private and public welfare field were involved.

176. GLABE, Donald B., FEIDER, Leo J., and PAGE, Harry O., "Reorientation for Treatment and Control," Pub. Welf., Apr. 1958, (Special Supplement I-XXIII).
   This project in Winona County, Minnesota, in which C.R.A. were active, attempts to find methods by which public welfare can control and prevent dependency, ill-health, and maladjustment. Administration and treatment are family-oriented, and case aides, home visiting policy, a revised eligibility procedure, and revised form recording were introduced as time-saving devices. Recommendations are made for an approach to m.p. families.

177. GRANT FOUNDATION, Modern Philanthropy and Human Welfare - A Round Table, Grant Foundation, New York City, 1952, 39 pp.
   Five experts from social work, public welfare, and public health discuss dependency,

maladjustment, and health in relation to some of the studies made by C.R.A. The discussions are related also to <u>Community Planning for Human Services</u> (see #129).

178. GRUNWALD, Hanna, "Group Counseling in Combating Delinquency," <u>Federal Probation</u>, Dec. 1958, 5 pp. (reprint available from Brooklyn Bureau of Social Service).
    A method of approaching the problem of delinquency of children of m.p. families through a group counseling program. This is one way in which social workers are trying new methods of working with the "hard core" client.

179. --------, "Group Counseling with the Multi-Problem Family," (in) <u>The Use of Group Techniques in the Family Agency</u>, Family Service Association of America, New York City, 1959, 31-42.
    Discussion of a program of group treatment of m.p. families. Case histories illustrate the various groups which received service, among them a group of socially deprived mothers, and a group of school-age boys. Procedures and techniques of group counseling are described, in relation to the m.p. family.

180. HAAS, Walter, "Reaching Out - A Dynamic Concept in Casework," <u>Soc. Wk.</u>, 4:3 (July 1959), 41-46.
    Discusses the "reaching out" process for voluntary and involuntary clients. The author points out the need for the client to know what the service is that is being offered to him, and the need for the worker to proceed at the pace of the client.

181. HALLINAN, Helen, "Co-ordinating Agency Efforts in Behalf of the Hard-to-Reach Family," <u>Soc. Casewk.</u>, 40:1 (Jan. 1959), pp. 9-17.
    The need for co-ordinating agency services on behalf of the hard-to-reach family is strongly emphasized.

182. HAWARTH, Elizabeth, "Definition and Diagnosis of the Social Problem Family," Soc. Wk., 10:1 (Jan. 1953), 765-768.

A picture of how problem families have been viewed throughout history. The author examines the various definitions of the problem family, and poses questions about the reason for its existence.

183. HARTMAN, Sara S., Problem Families in Public Housing, Baltimore, Maryland, Housing Authority, Baltimore, Maryland, 1956, 14 pp.

A condensation of an original 48-page report which summarizes the findings of a study of 355 problem families in 14 low-rent housing projects. The author briefly discusses the main difficulties which the families present, and points out ways of helping such families to integrate more positively in housing projects. Preventative service is emphasized.

184. HEALTH (THE) AND WELFARE COUNCIL OF THE BALTIMORE AREA, The Problem of the Domestic Relations Offender, Health and Welfare Council, Baltimore, Maryland, Nov. 1960, 68 pp.

Report of a study on the "domestic relations offender", undertaken in Baltimore. The most important of the proposals applies "the principle of preventative intervention for the protection of the community". The report recommends the setting up of "a new service unit" for the purpose of "aggressive community intervention" in chronically disorganized cases. This new service unit would use primarily an aggressive social casework approach, coupled with community organization and research. The casework would be family-unit centred, both in diagnosis and in treatment. The domestic relations offender and his family in Baltimore present the same type of problem as the families served in the St. Paul F.C.P.

185. HENRY, Charlotte S., "Motivation in Non-Voluntary Clients," Soc. Casewk., 39:2-3. (Feb.-Mar. 1958), 130-137.
    Discusses a project of the Family Service Association of Cleveland. A family-centred casework approach was used and included four processes: confrontation, reduction of fear, use of cultural expectation, and use of emotional support. Interviews were direct and of the "reaching out" type.

186. HILL, Reuben, "Social Stress on the Family - Generic Features of Families under Stress," Soc. Casewk., 39:2-3 (Feb.-Mar. 1958), 139-150.
    The author develops a four-fold classification of family crises, and describes them in relation to the lower-class family. He also discusses the impact of crisis, trouble, and stress on the family unit.

187. HILLMAN, Arthur, "Services to Multi-Problem Families," (in) Neighborhood Centers Today, National Federation of Settlements and Neighborhood Centers, New York City, 1960, 66-97.
    Description of work with m.p. families, from settlement-based services. It includes detailed descriptions of projects in Syracuse, New York City, Rochester, Columbus, and St. Paul.

188. --------, "Experimental Approaches in Deprived Areas," (in) Community Organization 1961, New York: Columbia University Press, 1961, 109-124.
    A short review of the many-pronged approach to m.p. families in which the author discusses the projects in Boston, New York, Detroit, Philadelphia, Rochester, and Syracuse. These are all experimental projects, usually centring in a settlement house.

189. HOFFMAN, William, "Offenders Have Families Too," C.C.C., St. Paul, Minnesota, 1958, 18 pp. (mimeo.).

A discussion of the criminal activity and background of a sample of 100 F.C.P. families. The author presents an approach to involving the whole family in treatment. The work of the single worker, who handles all problems, is reviewed, to show the validity of this approach to the m.p. family.

190. HOMMANN, Mary S., "New Haven Skid Row Rowhouses being Rehabilitated as Link in Renewal Chain," J. Housing, 18:8 (Aug.-Sept. 1961), 337-339.
    A description of a renewal project on Court Street in New Haven.

191. --------, "Neighborhood Rehabilitation is Working in Six Projects in New Haven; Here's How," J. Housing, 19:4 (May 1962), 185-193.
    An example of what can be done for families who formerly lived in substandard and dilapidated housing. This renewal project of Wooster Square in New Haven is a good example of how one community has begun action in the m.p. area.

192. ISH, Jefferson G., "The Aid to Dependent Children Program -- A Challenge to Negroes and Negro Leadership," Public Aid in Illinois, Oct. 1959, 5 pp. (reprint available from Illinois Public Aid Commission).
    A socio-cultural appraisal of dependency needs and problems of Negro families. The author discusses divorce, separation, desertion, and unmarried motherhood among the Negro population of the United States, and suggests certain approaches to these problems.

193. JOURNAL OF HOUSING, "Housing and Welfare Get Together," J. Housing, 19:3 (Mar.-Apr. 1962, Special Issue).
    The five articles discuss the relationship of social work to housing projects in Lafollette, St. Louis, Dallas, and Chicago.

This issue relates to m.p. families, who are frequently tenants of such projects.

194. ――――――, "Housing and Welfare," J. Housing, 13:3 (Mar. 1956, Special Issue).
A compilation of statements of theory and practice in the area of joint housing-welfare action to meet the problem family situation in public housing.

195. KASIUS, Cora, "Family Disorganization and the Multi-Problem Family," (in) Children and Youth in the 1960's, Golden Anniversary White House Conference on Children and Youth, Washington, D.C., 1960, 233-241 (Survey Papers).
An excellent review of knowledge about m.p. families in the United States. The following areas are covered: characteristics of the m.p. family; causal, social, and psychological factors; treatment methods; projects and new developments in the United States; techniques and procedures in dealing with m.p. families. The references include 60 items, which make a very good basic reading list for anyone interested in an American review of the m.p. family.

196. KOOS, Earl Lomon, Families in Trouble, New York: King's Crown Press, 1946, 134 pp.
A 2-year intensive study of 62 unbroken low-income families living in one New York City block. These families avoided contact with social agencies.

197. LAMPKIN, Lillian, and PODELL, Lawrence, Research Proposal: Evaluation of the Effect of Rehabilitation Services of a Municipal Interdepartmental Program upon Negro Multi-Problem Families, Interdepartmental Neighborhood Service Center, Office of the Mayor, New York City, 1962, 63 pp.
A proposed 3-year project for work with Negro m.p. families. It will include a description of the m.p. families and the programs of the agencies involved. The authors briefly review the definition of m.p. family and

the findings of the St. Paul F.C.P. study.
The study would take place in Central Harlem,
New York City, an area of 200,000 people, of
which 97 per cent are Negro. The Interdepartmental Neighborhood Service Center is a pilot
project and its staff is drawn from 4 municipal agencies (Department of Welfare, Board of
Education, Probation Department, Youth Board).
The program of this group is also detailed in
the proposal. The research design is spelled
out carefully. This thoroughly documented
proposal would be of especial value to communities who are planning systematic research
in the area of m.p. families.

198. LEADER, Arthur, "The Problem of Resistance in Social Work," Soc. Wk., 3:2 (Apr. 1958), 19-23.
An excellent analysis of the causes of client resistance in social casework. The author believes that resistance is a natural, healthy state of mind and that it can be coped with satisfactorily if the caseworker has a proper psychiatric understanding of the reasons for such resistance.

199. LEE, Rose Hum, "Multi-Problem Families of Maricopa County" (author's unpublished manuscript, Phoenix, Arizona, 1962, 92 pp.).
A report of a co-ordinated family casework unit working with m.p. families in Maricopa County, Arizona. Five social workers were each given a caseload of 40 cases. The 200 families in the project were of Spanish-Mexican, American Indian, Negro, White, and Asiatic ethnic backgrounds. A control group of 200 families who remained in the general caseload (368 cases to one worker) was also studied. The author used a 13-page schedule, which was filled out after nine months of service, to compare the two groups. Among her findings is the fact that the special unit closed more cases, but did not save any money. Recommendations are made for future approaches to service to m.p. families.

200. LEWIS, Hylan, "Child Rearing Practices Among Low-Income Families," (in) Casework Papers 1961, Family Service Association of America, New York City, 1961, 78-92.

   The author describes a study in Washington, D.C., which included 57 low-income families (49 non-White, 8 White), some of whom had characteristics of the m.p. family. He suggests that the m.p. family beset with problems of inadequacy, dependency, and neglect is a "clinical case" whose potential for rehabilitation is severely limited, and that research and demonstration programs should therefore be centred on the highly vulnerable family that is not yet clinically dependent or neglectful. We should examine the pre-clinical and sub-clinical aspects of dependency and neglect.

201. LINDENBERG, Ruth Ellen, "Hard to Reach: Client or Agency," Soc. Wk., 3:4 (Oct. 1958), 22-29.

   This article suggests the possibility that it is the agency which is hard to reach. She points out that the middle-class values of our agencies and social workers may stand in the way of successful work with m.p. families.

202. LIPPMAN, Hyman S., "Emotional Factors in Family Breakdown," Amer. J. Orthopsychiat., 24:3 (July 1954), 445-454.

   The author, a medical doctor, discusses the emotional factors in family breakdown, and relates them to some of the m.p. families in St. Paul and New York. Some of his remarks are related to the behaviour patterns of the children of these families, as well as to the neurotic patterns of the parents.

203. LOVE, Sidney, and MAYER, Herta, "Going Along with Defense in Resistive Families," Soc. Casewk., 40:2 (Feb. 1959), 69-74.

   Families can be helped if the worker understands their defenses and goes along with them. The article discusses how the social worker can handle and work with defenses in resistive families.

204. McCARTHY, Henry L., Report on the Activities of the Borough Committees of the Mayor's Interdepartmental Committee for Multi-Problem Families, Department of Welfare, New York City, 1958, 10 pp. (mimeo.).
Four Borough committees were set up to study m.p. families. A description of the characteristics of the families is given, and statistics illustrate the use of agency services for the 87 families in the study. The teamwork and co-ordination of agencies is fully summarized.

205. McCLARY, Howard C., "Volunteer Aids for Problem Ridden Families," Children, 8:5 (Sept.-Oct. 1961), 175-179.
Report of a pilot project using agency-trained and supervised volunteer case aids, in work with hard-to-reach families, at the Baden Street Settlement in Rochester, New York. Positive changes occurred among the families who were serviced by the volunteers. The overburdened staff of the agency were also helped by this unique use of specially trained volunteers.

206. McDOWELL, John, "Seeing the Family Whole," Public Aid in Illinois, 1:3 (Feb. 1959), 13 pp.
The author discusses some of the many forms, facets, and functions of the family; then outlines the need for teamwork among agencies and among social workers in their planning for m.p. families.

207. McKIBBIN, Beatrice, "Social Services for Public Housing," J. Housing, 17:10 (Nov. 1960), 411-416.
Review of the co-ordination of community services in a public housing project in Syracuse, New York, for m.p. families.

208. McKIBBIN, Beatrice, and CARY, Lee J., "A Family Consultation Service in Public Housing," Youth Development Center, Syracuse, New York, 1961, 10 pp. (mimeo.).
Paper delivered at the National Conference on Social Welfare in Minneapolis. The authors discuss a demonstration program in a housing project of 678 units, which contains

many m.p. families. Of families in the project, 54 were of the m.p. type. An analysis of these families is briefly given. The authors also discuss "a case contact chart" which was developed in the process of working with these families.

209. McLAIN, Osborne, "Social Work in a Public Housing Project," Soc. Casewk., 41:8 (Oct. 1960), 408-413.
Discussion of the work done in the Philadelphia Housing Project. Case illustrations are included in the description of social work and other community resources dealing with a small core of m.p. families.

210. MEIER, Gitta, "The Effect of Unwanted Pregnancies on a Relief Load," Eugenics Quarterly, 8:3 (Sept. 1961), 142-153.
A detailed examination of 25 multi-problem families in which an unwanted pregnancy took place. The author discusses the definition, incidence and implications of unwanted pregnancies. She feels that this type of pregnancy is due to "lack of, or inadequate, motivation". (See also a condensed version of article in Social Work, 6:2 (April 1961), 114-116.)

211. MILLER, Walter B., "Cultural Factors of an Urban Lower Class Community," National Institute of Mental Health, Community Services Branch, Silver Spring, Maryland, 1962, 47 pp. (mimeo., to be published).
An excellent description of lower class culture, of importance to social workers working with m.p. families. The author points out the differences of the middle class values of the social worker and the divers patterns of lower class groups. (See also Social Service Review, 33:3 (Sept. 1959), 219-236.)

212. MILWAUKEE (CITY OF), "Mayor's Study Committee on Social Problems in the Inner Core Area of the City" (Final Report), Milwaukee, Wisconsin, Apr. 15, 1960, 100 pp.(mimeo.).
This is a comprehensive, detailed report

on the social problems in the inner core
area of Milwaukee. Most pertinent is Annex
J: "Report of Committee on Problem Families
in the Inner Core". This section includes a
definition of m.p. families and a series of
recommendations for changes in legislation
and health and welfare services, improvements
in existing services, and research.

213. MINNESOTA STATE WELFARE CONFERENCE, "The Family Centered Project of St. Paul through the Workers' Eyes," C.C.C., St. Paul, Minnesota, 1959, 22 pp. (mimeo.).
Panel discussion of the co-operative effort of seven agencies in St. Paul, in regard to the m.p. families project. An honest look at inter-agency co-operation, especially in the private-public agency sphere.

214. NAHRO PUBLICATION, Community Services and Public Housing, National Association of Housing and Redevelopment Officials, Washington, D.C., 1961, 16 pp.
This pamphlet contains the seven major recommendations made by the subcommittee on Community Services and Public Housing. The recommendations are geared towards co-operative efforts on behalf of the tenants of housing projects, among whom many m.p. families can be found. For each recommendation, a justification is set out. There is also a statement of principles on the role of the social worker in public housing and urban renewal programs.

215. ---------, Change for the Better, National Association of Housing and Redevelopment Officials, Washington, D.C., 1962, 102 pp.
A collection of papers dealing with housing projects and their relation to family life. Many of the projects involve m.p. families in slum-type housing which is being changed into more adequate housing. This document was assembled by the Committee on Social Work in Housing and Urban Renewal. The housing projects described by various

authors are located in Baltimore, Boston, Pittsburgh, Portland, Rochester, Chicago, Cincinatti, Detroit, Milwaukee, New York, and Syracuse. The book has a 31-item annotated bibliography on the use of social work skills in housing and urban renewal.

216. NEUHAUS, Ruby, "Family Treatment in Focus," Marr. Fam. Living, 24:1 (Feb. 1962), 62-65.

    An approach used by the Lutheran Welfare Society of Minnesota in working with families as a unit. It is assumed that family treatment can be used if some meaningful family ties exist.

217. NEW HAVEN COUNCIL OF SOCIAL AGENCIES, Neighborhood Improvement Project, Council of Social Agencies, New Haven, Connecticut, 1960, 12 pp.

    Annual report of the first year of operation of the Neighborhood Improvement Project (N.I.P.), New Haven, Connecticut. The N.I.P. is a program directed toward families with school-age children (ages 5-16 inclusive), where the children are "in clear and present danger". The program incorporates: family-centred casework, community service, neighbourhood organization, and research. All of these four aspects are reported on. Also included are: the goals for the second year of operation, and the system for classifying the relationship of the client to the N.I.P. worker.

218. NEW YORK CITY CHAPTER NATIONAL ASSOCIATION OF SOCIAL WORKERS, Multi-Problem Families and Casework Practice, N.Y.C.N.A.S.W., New York City, 1960, 7 pp.

    Report of a subcommittee to study casework practices with m.p. families. Three main characteristics of constructive attitude, acceptance of realistic goals, and sound diagnosis and treatment are discussed in this report.

219. NEW YORK CITY YOUTH BOARD, Reaching the Unreached, New York City Youth Board, New York City, 1952, 151 pp.
    The first publication of size to present the experimental and courageous program of the Youth Board. Twelve authorities in social work discuss such topics as reaching out to families, aggressive casework, group psychotherapy, teen-age gangs, and the programs of various social agencies to help the family who has not been reached before.

220. --------, Reaching the Unreached Family, New York City Youth Board, New York City, 1958, 54 pp. (Monograph No. 5).
    A study of 150 m.p. families, which includes a quantitative study of the characteristics of these families. Eight case illustrations show the type of service offered to the families in the study. This was a "reaching out" effort on the part of the social workers of the Youth Board.

221. NEW YORK STATE CHARITIES AID ASSOCIATION, Multi-Problem Families: A New Name or a New Problem?, Social Research Service, State Charities Aid Association, New York City, 1960, 25 pp.
    The first part of this report deals with comments on m.p. families, which include definitions and approaches. The second part includes summaries of projects with such families in Buffalo, Munroe County, Rochester, Elmira, Syracuse, Oneida County, and New York City.

222. --------, Health and Welfare Needs in New York State, State Charities Aid Association, New York City, 1960, 40 pp.
    A survey report of health and welfare needs in the 57 counties of Upstate New York. One of the highest needs found was for interagency collaboration about m.p. families. Fact-finding about these families also ranked high. The respondents to the questionnaire consistently pointed out that additional

services or facilities for m.p. families are not needed, but more effective focusing of existing resources, and co-ordinated services for these families, are of high priority.

223. NOLES, John Davis, "The Problems and Needs of 'Hard to Reach' Families: A Challenge to the Community (unpublished Master's thesis, School of Social Welfare, Louisiana State University, 1961).
The author studied ten m.p. families known to the East Baton Rouge Parish Family Court. His study included case record reading and personal interviews with each family. Present approaches to these families appeared inadequate. The author predicts a generational pattern unless these families are "reached".

224. NORMAN, F. M., "The Skills Needed for Work with Problem Families," Soc. Wk., 10:1 (Jan. 1953), 764-765.
A description of how homemaking services can be taught to improve the homecraft standards of mothers with poor facilities.

225. OJEMANN, Ralph H. (ed.), Recent Research Looking Toward Preventive Intervention, Iowa City: State University of Iowa, 1961, 200 pp.
This publication reports the proceedings of the Third Institute on Preventive Psychiatry (other two also available from same source). There are three chapters, which are relevant to work with m.p. families. Dr. Erich Lindemann discusses preventive intervention in social and emotional crises; Dr. Wells Goodrich summarizes recent research in early family development and personality; and Dr. Kral reviews research in prevention of mental disorders. Each major paper is followed by discussions. The members of the Institute come from allied professions in the mental health field.

226. OPPENHEIMER, Hannah, "Case Conferences in a Family Center," <u>Children</u>, 9:6 (Nov.-Dec. 1962), 232-237.
    An example of the procedure used in a case conference on a problem family serviced by the Huntington Family Centers in Syracuse. The author reviews the case history, and summarizes the conference, which included participating social agencies focusing on the total family group.

227. ORMSBY, Ralph, "Defining the Problem Family," <u>Soc. Wk.</u>, 4:1 (Jan. 1959), 109.
    The author feels that the term "hard to reach" is not an exclusive term which defines the severe problem family, and feels that the term "multi-problem family" is too unspecific to be used for study purposes. A new more scientific term is needed, or a more compassionate term.

228. OVERTON, Alice. "Servicing Families Who Don't Want Help," <u>Soc. Casewk.</u>, 34:7 (July 1953), 304-309.
    Families who were in greatest need, and were of highest cost to the community, were chosen for this project in New York City. The families were approached on the basis of concern for the children. The author discusses the approach to these families in detail.

229. --------, "The Workers' Seminar - A Group Approach to Professional Development," C.C.C., St. Paul, Minnesota, 1957, 10 pp. (mimeo.).
    A talk to the Conference of Jewish Communal Welfare, which summarizes the activities of the Workers' Seminar of the twelve caseworkers of the F.C.P., under the chairmanship of the author. The article explores the value of such a group process, to aid workers in a new and difficult experience.

230. ---------, "Resistance in Serving Families at Odds with the Community," C.C.C., St. Paul, Minnesota, 1957, 12 pp. (mimeo.).
   The paper describes the feelings of social workers who meet resistance from families who do not want intrusion in their lives. The author makes suggestions as to the qualities needed for such social workers. Case illustrations are given.

231. ---------, "Clients' Observations of Social Work," C.C.C., St. Paul, Minnesota, 1959, 22 pp. (mimeo.).
   Excerpts from twelve hours of tape recording of a small group of 13 people from m.p. families, who came to four group meetings to discuss their reactions and feelings at being serviced by social workers in the F.C.P. The responses are very honest and candid, and indicate the real feelings of many families who are dependent on social work help.

232. ---------, "Taking Help from Our Clients," Soc. Wk., 5:2 (Apr. 1960), 42-50.
   Clients of the St. Paul F.C.P. were asked their opinions about the work of their social workers. The clients were very honest about expressing their feelings. A summary of what a good worker should be, according to the clients, is included in this article.

233. OVERTON, Alice, and TINKER, Katherine H., Casework Notebook, C.C.C., St. Paul, Minnesota, 1959, 174 pp.
   The first section of this book discusses in general terms the m.p. families in the F.C.P. in St. Paul. Section 2 reviews the approaches to the families used by the social workers. The third part deals with such topics as family interviewing, role of the social worker, and the lessons learned from the project. The appendix contains an outline for social diagnosis, and a bibliography of 33 items used in discussions in the workers' seminars of the F.C.P.

234. PAGE, Harry O., "Progress Toward Control of Dependency," <u>Pub. Welf.</u>, 14:4 (Oct. 1956), 200-206.
   Interim report on developments and findings in the Winona, Minnesota, project which was focused on the prevention and reduction of dependency in the public assistance program. Services to family units are stressed in this study.

235. PAGE, Harry O., and AXELROD, S. J., "Community Teamwork by Public Health and Welfare," <u>Pub. Welf.</u>, 12:2 (Apr. 1955), 53-57.
   "This article is intended to describe experimental work in several American communities, which is currently testing our thesis that integrated teamwork to match interrelated human problems can set us on the road to prevention and control of our communities' most burdensome human problems." The article outlines the plan and goals of four local projects: in Winona (Minnesota), Washington County (Hagerstown, Maryland), San Mateo (California), and the St. Paul Family Centered Project.

236. PAGE, Miriam O., "Cohesion, Dignity and Hope for Multi-Problem Families," <u>Children</u>, 8:2 (Mar.-Apr. 1962), 63-69.
   Review of a demonstration project to help 37 m.p. families active with the Vermont Department of Social Welfare. Services include casework, home visiting, neighbourhood clubs, and improvement projects. Families gained by this approach.

237. PAGET, Norman, and KERN, Marcella R., <u>Counselling Services to Parents and Children Involved in Divorce Proceedings</u>, Family Service Agency, San Bernardino, California, July 1960, 80 pp.
   Report of a reaching-out counseling service to parents and their children involved in divorce proceedings. Some cases were of m.p. family types. Case illustrations are used to show how the "reaching-out" service

was used.

238. PARAD, Howard J., and CAPLAN, Gerald, "A Framework for Studying Families in Crisis," Soc. Wk., 5:3 (July 1960), 3-16.
   The authors present an approach to the observation and study of the family in crisis, using a case illustration. Their conceptual framework includes "preventive intervention" as part of the casework approach.

239. PHILADELPHIA PUBLIC WELFARE DEPARTMENT, "An Evaluative Analysis of Family Service as Provided by the Division of Youth Conservation Services," Department of Public Welfare, Philadelphia, Pennsylvania, May 1960, 10 pp. (mimeo.).
   A pilot project in working with children of 301 m.p. families. The characteristics of these children were that they averaged 4 police contacts per year, and at least one police contact within 45 days of the family's acceptance for service. The characteristics of the m.p. families are discussed and statistically illustrated. One major conclusion is that the number of police contacts decrease when families receive intensive casework service.

240. RAPPAPORT, Mazie F., "Clarifying the Service to Families with Many Problems," J. Soc. Wk. Process, 11 (1960), 77-87.
   This article is part of the annual volume published by the Alumni Association and Faculty of the University of Pennsylvania School of Social Work. The author discusses two m.p. family cases, and asks many questions which face social workers as they work with the compounded problems of such families. (See also #74, 77, 82 in same journal.)

241. REGENSBERG, Jeanette, "Reaching Children before the Crisis Comes," Soc. Casewk., 35:3 (Mar. 1954), 104-111.
   The subject of this paper concerns "those children who are vulnerable to

breakdown in emotional health (in delinquency or illness) when parents are unwilling or unable to seek help". Some of the topics covered are: mobilization for prevention; a reinterpretation of social responsibility; who are the hard-to-reach parents; guarded parents; social-work-shy parents; and some of the demands on the worker.

242. REINER, Beatrice Simcox, and KAUFMAN, Irving, Character Disorders in Parents of Delinquents, Family Service Association of America, New York City, 1959, 179 pp.
    Fifteen cases from the files of Judge Baker Guidance Center in Boston illustrate the various character disorders found in parents. The authors discuss treatment in four stages: establishing a relationship, ego-building through identification, helping the client establish a separate identity, and helping the client gain self-understanding. Chapters 9 and 10 are especially relevant to work with m.p. families, whose adult members exhibit many character disorders. The last chapter discusses a community approach to reduce family pathology.

243. ROACH, Jack, "Helping Families Who Don't Want Help," Pub. Welf., 17:2 (Apr. 1959), 61-67.
    Discussion of a project in Niagara Falls, New York, in work with 44 m.p. families. The family-centred approach is used, and the article is illustrated with case material.

244. ROBINSON, Marion O., "A Team Approach in Preventing Maladjustment," Children, 2:2 (Mar.-Apr. 1955), 69-73.
    Short discussion of the C.R.A. study in San Mateo County, California. The author briefly summarizes the findings of other C.R.A. studies on m.p. families. The team approach is suggested for tackling the problems of these families.

245. ――――――, "Community-Wide Planning for Family Health and Welfare," Marr. Fam. Living, 19:2 (May 1957), 198-203.
    The intertwining nature of multiple problems within a family group demands an integrated approach on the part of various services and disciplines. The author discusses this aspect in relation to four community studies by C.R.A.

246. ROBINSON, Ruth, "Description of a Case Aide Program in a Multi-Function Agency," Bureau of Social Service, Brooklyn, New York, 1961, 16 pp. (mimeo.).
    A good account of the use of case aides in various aspects of the agency program, including work with m.p. families. The author outlines the development of the plan, and discusses the detailed job of case aides who are university graduates but not social workers. This paper is especially important to agencies who find that existing social work staff spends too much time on clerical and service items rather than casework service.

247. ROCHESTER AND MUNROE COUNTY COUNCIL OF SOCIAL AGENCIES, Local Approaches to the Multi-Problem Family, Rochester and Munroe County Council of Social Agencies, Rochester, New York, May 1958, 16 pp.
    A review of the local developments of approaches to the m.p. family situation in the County. It includes work with families in housing projects. Suggestions for further co-operation are made.

248. ――――――, Report on Hard-to-Reach Multi-Problem Families, Rochester and Munroe County Council of Social Agencies, Rochester, New York, Nov. 1958, 13 pp. (mimeo.).
    The report by the Family and Children's Division of the Council deals mainly with recommendations for the study and treatment of the families. Recommendations in the area of education, recreation, housing, social services, treatment services, and financing are

made.

249. ROGERS, Muriel Nelson, "A Group Educational Program for Marginally Adjusted Families," Soc. Casewk., 53:4 (Apr. 1962), 178-184.
   A description of family life education provided by the Jewish Family Service of New York to a group of tenants who were chronically tardy in paying their rent to the New York City Housing Authority.

250. RONEY, Jay L., "Special Stresses on Low Income Families," Soc. Casewk., 39:2-3 (Feb.-Mar. 1958), 150-158.
   The article centres on the stresses which affect persons known to public welfare agencies, and makes suggestions for alleviating needs and stresses of low-income families.

251. ROWAN, Carl T., "Is There Hope for Hopeless Families?," Saturday Evening Post, July 5, 1958, 5 pp. (reprint available from C.R.A.).
   A popularly written article about the St. Paul F.C.P. It is illustrated by the hardest of the "hard-core families" who presented a lot of problems to the police. The article also traces the beginning of the F.C.P., and terminates with a case illustration of a family whom the F.C.P. helped.

252. SAMUELS, Gertrude, "Plans to Salvage the Problem Family," New York Times Magazine, May 12, 1957, 17 pp.
   Description of the controlled experiment in New York City in the Chelsea district of Manhatten. The author discusses the m.p. families, with special emphasis on the high delinquency rates found among children of these families. The "Hudson Guild", a social agency, is in the forefront to help families in this area.

253. --------, "To Brighten the Gray Areas'", New York Times Magazine, Oct. 22, 1961, 48 pp.
   A discussion of the Bloomingdale Area

on the West Side in New York City, which contains many m.p. families. The author describes a project initiated to clear up some of the many difficulties found in this area.

254. ---------, "A Walk along the Worst Block," The New York Times Magazine, Section 6, Part 1, Sept. 30, 1962, 18-19, 84-85.
A description of life in 100th St. between 1st and 2nd Avenue in New York's Spanish Harlem. Many of the families living in this area can be termed m.p. families. This is a vivid account of the environment, socio-economic influences, and the attempts at rehabilitation made in this area. The drug problem appears to be a major one for youngsters of this block. The city is now attempting to do something about this area.

255. SCHEIDLINGER, Saul, "Experimental Group Treatment of Severely Deprived Latency-Age Children," Amer. J. Orthopsychiat., 30:2 (Apr. 1960), 356-368.
A well documented account of group treatment of children of m.p. families. About 90 per cent of the children came from Negro homes, and their families were serviced by a non-sectarian family service agency in New York. The author uses frequent case illustrations to show the effect of group treatment on these children. Observations on the therapeutic possibilities of such a group are included in the article.

256. SCHEIDLINGER, Saul, and PYRKE, Marjorie, "Group Therapy of Women with Severe Dependency Problems," Amer. J. Orthopsychiat., 31:4 (Oct. 1961), 776-785.
This paper covers an experimental group therapy approach with women who come from m.p. families. The authors had 50 weekly sessions with 8 Negro women, each with 3 or more children. Through case illustrations the progress of these group therapy sessions is traced. The value of group treatment is discussed fully. The clients were all ser-

viced by the Community Service Society of
New York.

257. SCHERZ, Frances, "What Is Family Centered
Casework," <u>Soc. Casewk.</u>, 34:8 (Oct. 1953),
343-349.
    The author defines and discusses family-
centred casework. This approach has been
used by many agencies lately in their work
with m.p. families.

258. SHERMAN, Sanford N., "Joint Interviews in Casework Practice," <u>Soc. Wk.</u>, 4:2 (Apr. 1959),
20-28.
    The author outlines the methodology of
conducting interviews in social casework practice with the whole family. The techniques
described in the paper should be helpful in
dealing with m.p. families.

259. SIMMONS, Harold E., and others, <u>Teamwork in
Services for Rehabilitation in Public
Assistance</u>, American Public Welfare Association, Chicago, Illinois, 1957, 16 pp.
    The purpose of this pamphlet is to con-
vey the values to be realized from teamwork
among three kinds of services: (1) casework
services; (2) medical and psychiatric services; (3) vocational counseling and employment services.

260. SOYER, David, "Reaching Problem Families
through Settlement-Based Casework," <u>Soc.
Wk.</u>, 6:3 (July 1961), 36-43.
    The author describes the work done at
the Manhattenville Community Centers in New
York City. Case illustrations show the
settlement-based casework approach to "hard
to reach" clients.

261. STAFF OF THE F.C.P., "What Are We Up To In
St. Paul?," C.C.C., St. Paul, Minnesota,
1955, 29 pp. (mimeo.).
    A talk to the Twin City Chapter of the
American Association of Social Workers by
the staff of the F.C.P., reviewing the

background and structure, the approach, the family-centred focus, and the use of the social worker in treatment, in the F.C.P.

262. STAR, Jack, "A Way Out of Our Welfare Dead End," Look, May 8, 1962, 3 pp. (reprint available from C.R.A.).
    A popular article based on the St. Paul F.C.P. The author illustrates his story with three case histories.

263. STINSON, Malcolm, "Family Centered Project of St. Paul: An Experience in Community Organization," C.C.C., St. Paul, Minnesota, 1956, 15 pp. (mimeo.).
    Planning in social work is primarily a problem of human relations. The F.C.P. experience confirms the value of the experimental approach to finding the answers on a community-wide basis.

264. STONE, Edward, ZILBACH, Joan J., HURWITZ, Jacob I., and IDELSON, Roberta, The Place in Darkness, United Community Services, Boston, Massachusetts, 1962, 3 volumes, 621 pp. (unpublished).
    Since 1956 an attempt had been made to work with chronic families through the Chronic Family Project in Boston. The three-volume report details some of the case histories of the families in the project, and examines the frustrations, accomplishments, and steps in this project. The family-centred approach is clearly documented in warm and human non-professional language. Volume 3 contains the minutes and proceedings of the project. One of the very few documents which have looked at the chronic family in such personal and minute terms.

265. STRAUS, Murray A., Family Measurement Abstracts, University of Minnesota Family Study Center, Minneapolis, Minnesota, 1961, 250 pp. (mimeo.).
    A compendium of abstracts and classification of existing techniques for measuring

family behaviour. Instruments (127) used to study family behaviour are abstracted. The author hopes that this material will stimulate the development of new or improved techniques. Each abstract lists the test used, the author, variables measured, test description, sample item, evidence of validity, sample, reliability, length, norms, and references about the use of the test.

266. STRICKLER, Evelyn, "Helping the Multi-Problem Family through a Coordination of Services in a Predominantly Rural Setting," Child Welf., 41:1 (Jan. 1962), 22-28.
Using case illustrations, the author describes the development of co-ordinated services to m.p. families in a rural setting. The emphasis is on "reaching out" on the part of agencies.

267. SVIHUS, Richard H., "Health and Social Agency Use at a Naval Training Center," Amer. J. Pub. Health, 52:2 (Feb. 1962), 200-207.
An application of the St. Paul study findings of m.p. families to 3,783 naval recruits. The multi-use by the naval recruits of four services (health and social services, dispensaries, neuro-psychiatric unit, chaplains and line officers) was studied. Of the population, 8.8 per cent made use of the services of three or more of the four agencies. They made use of half of the visits to chaplains and disciplinary agencies, one-fourth of visits to the psychiatric agency, and one-fifth of visits to the health agency. The author concludes that for some of these recruits a fairly accurate prediction of their problems and use of service could be made by means of a routine psychiatric screening device.

268. SYRACUSE UNIVERSITY, "Aid for Multi-Problem Families," Youth Development Center Reports, Winter 1961, 6-8.
An interview with Janet Weinandy, social worker for the Family Consultation Service,

which works with m.p. families in a Syracuse public housing project. The discussion covers work with 56 such families, and discusses the approaches used.

269. TERRESBERRY, Shirley, Family Casework in Royal Oak Township, Family Service of Oakland County, Detroit, Michigan, 1962, 22 pp. (mimeo.).
An analysis of 82 m.p. family cases in two areas of metropolitan Detroit. Royal Oak Township families were all Negro, while Pontiac families were 90 per cent White. The socio-economic backgrounds of both sets of m.p. families are presented. The author also presents social pathology, referral sources, problems of clients, mental health status and characteristics of service given. The goals and effectiveness of service are enumerated. This study is important to communities where racial groups are changing neighbourhoods in a rapid manner and creating new m.p. family patterns.

270. TINKER, Katherine H., Let's Look At Our Failures, C.C.C., St. Paul, Minnesota, 1957, 43 pp.
An examination of 7 F.C.P. families, who could not be helped. The author gives us family profiles, and discusses family-centred treatment processes.

271. ---------, Patterns of Family Centered Treatment, C.C.C., St. Paul, Minnesota, 1959, 43 pp.
A descriptive study of 30 F.C.P. closed cases. The author gives us the characteristics of the m.p. families, and discusses fully the treatment approach including the casework contacts. The use of community resources is also illustrated. The appendix contains a sample schedule which was used to tabulate data for this study.

272. ---------, "Casework with Hard-to-Reach Families," Amer. J. Orthopsychiat., 29:1 (Jan. 1959), 165-171.

A discussion of the casework approach in the F.C.P. in St. Paul. It is documented with case material from the clients and the social workers in the project. Casework skills for hard-to-reach families is a new concept, which has been successfully tried in St. Paul.

273. TUCKER, Dorothy, "Value of a Child Guidance Clinic to a County" (author's unpublished speech, Platteville, Wisconsin, July 22, 1957, 4 pp.).
The author illustrates vividly the immense human and material costs of two m.p. families in the county. One family alone received $58,700 as Aid to Dependent Children allowance during 14 years of dependency. The author calculates that the total cost for this family will reach $150,000 in tax money, which includes help to all members of this family.

274. UNITED COMMUNITY COUNCIL OF COLUMBUS, "Excerpts from Report to Multi-Problem Family Research Project Committee," United Community Council, Columbus, Ohio, Mar. 23, 1960, 13 pp. (mimeo.).
This publication is based on an M.S.W. thesis: "A Study of the Social Disorganization, Criminal Records and Involvement with Social Welfare Agencies of Fifty Families from the Franklin County Juvenile Court Caseload". Characteristics of the families are presented, findings analyzed briefly, and recommendations for dealing with m.p. families in the Columbus area are presented.

275. UNITED COMMUNITY FUNDS AND COUNCILS OF AMERICA, "Inter-Agency Communication in New Haven, Connecticut," United Community Funds and Councils of America, Inc., New York City, Jan. 1958, 47 pp. (mimeo.).
A pilot research study which involved the casework, supervisory, and executive personnel of 15 agencies operating in the social adjustment field.

276. ——————, "Citizens Conference on Community Planning 1961" (Summaries of Round Tables), United Community Funds and Councils of America, New York City, 1961, 5 pp.

These summaries discuss the services offered to families in public housing projects in Boston, Jefferson County, Washington, D.C., and Stamford. Introduction of social workers into these projects seemed to help families with their problems.

277. UNITED COMMUNITY SERVICES OF BOSTON, Roxbury Projects, United Community Services, Boston, Massachusetts, Report #1, 1957, 8 pp; Report #2, 1958, 4 pp.

The Roxbury Family Project of Boston, Massachusetts, has been in existence since October 1956. An outgrowth of the Roxbury Youth Project (which was a 3-year demonstration program, using a community approach to juvenile delinquency), the Family Project is directed toward m.p. families in the Roxbury area. It is the co-operative effort of the United Community Services and five family agencies. Some of the purposes of the project: improvement of the understanding of m.p. families; improvement in methods of service; development of more efficient interagency co-operation and service.

278. ——————, "Chronic Problem Family Care Project," United Community Services, Boston, Massachusetts, 1960, 4 pp. (mimeo.).

A definition of the m.p. family in relation to this project (Roxbury Project) is given, together with a description of the program involving 27 families. The research design is briefly reviewed.

279. VOILAND, Alice L., Family Casework Diagnosis, C.R.A., New York City, Nov. 1961, 18 pp.

The author discusses a research project, in which she classifies disordered family types as: (1) perfectionist family, (2) inadequate family, (3) egocentric family, and (4) unsocial family. Each type is described in detail. Her sample was taken from C.R.A.'s projects on work with m.p. families. (See #280 below.)

280. VOILAND, Alice L., and BUELL, Bradley, "A Classification of Disordered Family Types," Soc. Wk., 6:4 (Oct. 1961), 3-11.
The following "disordered family types" are described: perfectionist family, inadequate family, egocentric family, and the unsocial family. Characteristics of each type are given, and a prognosis for each type is made.

281. VOILAND, Alice L., and ASSOCIATES, Family Casework Diagnosis, New York: Columbia University Press, 1962, 369 pp.
An eight-year study of 888 cases carried by community-supported health and welfare agencies. Includes classifications of psychosocial disorders and of disordered family types, and a framework for diagnostic analysis and synthesis of family social functioning. The cases were selected from C.R.A. projects.

282. WAGNER, Nathanial N., "Developmental Aspects of Impulse Control," Journal of Consulting Psychology, 2:6 (1960), 537-540.
This study investigated the relationship of family pathology, as measured by Block and Behrens Multi-Problem Family Index, and the level of impulse control in 36 children (residents of the Astor Home for Children, a treatment and research centre for emotionally disturbed boys). The presence of family pathology was found to be significantly associated with low impulse control, the absence of family pathology with high impulse control. It is suggested that contact, and probably identification, with pathological parental figures hinders the development of impulse control.

283. WALKER, Gerald, "An Answer to Juvenile Delinquency," Cosmopolitan, Nov. 1957, 4 pp. (reprint available from C.R.A.).

A discussion of juvenile delinquency in relation to the m.p. families studied by C.R.A. in the F.C.P. in St. Paul.

284. WARREN, Roland L., and SMITH, Jesse, "Report on the Chemung County (Elmira) New York Project of Casework Service to Chronically Dependent Multi-Problem Families," State Charities Aid Association, New York City, 1962, 17 pp. (mimeo.).
Paper given at the National Conference on Social Welfare. The project involves intensive family-centred casework by highly qualified caseworkers with a small number of m.p. families. The authors discuss the characteristics of an acceptable research design for impact evaluation, and review the difficulties in implementing the project in the community. Statistics are not included.

285. WEINANDY, Janet E., Families Under Stress, Youth Development Center, Syracuse, New York, 1962, 20 pp.
Report on the first year of a 3-year Family Consultation Service in public housing. The purpose is to test the effectiveness of a short-term, intensive social service program for 24 of the m.p. families living in a public housing project in Syracuse.

286. WELFARE COUNCIL OF METROPOLITAN CHICAGO, Breaking Through Barriers, Welfare Council, Chicago, Illinois, 1960, 129 pp.
Report on the Hard-to-Reach Youth Project. Chapters 4, 7, and 8 are especially pertinent to the problem of m.p. families. They deal with values of the community, interagency co-operation, and contain recommendations.

287. ————, Aid to Dependent Children: Facts, Fallacies, Future, Welfare Council, Chicago, Illinois, 1962, 48 pp.
Summary of the two-volume report published by Greenleigh Associates. Aid to Dependent Children families in Cook County,

Illinois, are described, and appear to have characteristics in common with m.p. families. Four pilot projects, which attempted to rehabilitate this type of family, are reviewed and many misconceptions, untruths, and stereotypes about these families are cleared up in this report. Suggestions are made for strengthening the whole Aid to Dependent Children program on the local, state, and national level. (Complete report from Greenleigh Associates, 437 Fifth Ave., New York City.)

288. WHALE, Margaret, "The Problem Family - The Case for Social Casework," Soc. Wk., 11:1 (Jan. 1954), 881-887.
   The author outlines the symptoms, definition, and attitudes of 8 problem families, and discusses the casework method in relation to these families.

289. WHELAN, Ralph, "Changed Approaches to the Unreached," Children, 2:3 (May-June 1953), 105-110.
   A short review of the "new" approaches used to reach m.p. families and "resisting" clients. It includes agency teamwork, aggressive casework, and group work and recreation. The author is Director of the New York City Youth Board.

290. WILLIE, Charles V., "The Structure and Composition of 'Problem' and 'Stable' Families in a Lower Income Population," Youth Development Center, Syracuse, New York, 1962, 15 pp. (mimeo.).
   A discussion of the difference between problem and stable families. The author looks at marriage, child-rearing patterns, marital status, in order to compare the two groups found in a housing project in Syracuse (see #285). The author suggests that behaviour of m.p. families is "uncontrolled" and that they are "uncommitted". The author, an anthropologist, applies some of Malinowski's findings to his own hypothesis.

291. WILLIE, Charles V., WAGENFELD, Morton O., and CARY, Lee J., "The Effect of Social Service upon Rental-Paying Patterns of Low-Income Problem Families," Youth Development Center, Syracuse, New York, 1962, 19 pp. (submitted for publication).
　　The authors examine the rental-paying patterns of problem families in a public housing project in Syracuse. Fifty-four families were identified in this housing project. The project emphasizes the significant role of the social worker as "intercessor in fostering change in a social system". The paper illustrates the positive use of a social worker (family consultant) in a housing project.

292. WILTSE, Kermit, "The Hopeless Family," Soc. Wk., 3:6 (Oct. 1958), 12-22.
　　A definition of the "hopeless family" is given. The author discusses the characteristics of this type of family, and suggests approaches for social workers. He emphasizes ego-support and ego-building, and feels that "Love is not enough".

293. WOOD, Elizabeth, The Small Hard Core, Citizens Housing and Planning Council, New York City, 1957, 26 pp.
　　A study of 109 problem families at St. Nicholas public housing project in Manhattan. The author discusses the problems, agency services, and social work programs for this group of families. The role of public housing is outlined and recommendations are made to implement aid to such families. The appendix contains a statistical presentation of the characteristics of the problem families.

MISCELLANEOUS

(Items received too late to permit classification)

294. AIDE À TOUTE DÉTRESSE, Famille*s inadaptées et relations humaines*, Aide à Toute Détresse, Paris, 1961, 130 pp. (Premiere Partie).
     This is the first volume of the proceedings of a U.N.E.S.C.O. sponsored seminar on the m.p. family in Paris on May 12-14, 1961. The proceedings were edited by the Social Research Bureau of the Aide à Toute Détresse. This volume contains eight papers which deal with the social, sociological, psychological, legal, biological, and spiritual needs and problems of the m.p. family. Seven of the papers are given by French experts, and one on "Human Relations and the Problem Family" is by A. F. Philp of Great Britain.

295. ---------, Familles inadaptées: leur logement, leur travail, Aide à Toute Détresse, Paris, 1961, 114 pp. (Deuxieme Partie).
     Volume Two deals with the housing and employment of m.p. families. Six papers dealing with the housing problem are from German, Dutch, French, and Spanish sources. Employment problems are dealt with in four papers from Holland and France. Principal conclusions and recommendations follow each of the two main sections.

296. DEBUYST, Renard G., and RACINE, A., Quatre monographies de familles-problèmes, Centre d'Étude de la Delinquance Juvenile, Brussels, 1962 (Publication No. 9), 140 pp.
     The Centre for Study of Juvenile Delinquency was established in 1957 to investigate the problem of the "failure of paternal authority" in many families, resulting in court action on behalf of the children. The present study is an intensive examination, by the use of comprehensive case records, of four large problem families living in the

district of Mons, Belgium, a mining district which has been declining economically since 1930. The authors give complete histories of the families, with special emphasis on the family background of the parents as well as of the children, and methods of approach are described. The centre has published ten monographs on delinquency, of which seven are in French and three in Flemish.

297. GREENLEIGH ASSOCIATES, Facts, Fallacies and Future, Greenleigh Associates Inc., New York City, 1960, 100 pp.
Report of a study of 1,010 families who are receiving help through the Aid to Dependent Children Program in Cook County, Illinois. These families do not have their fathers living in the home. The findings are relevant to m.p. families, since some of the characteristics of the families and the attitude of the community are similar.

298. --------, Addenda to Facts, Fallacies and Future, Greenleigh Associates Inc., New York City, 1960, 148 pp.
The Addenda examines in detail the characteristics of these families, and discusses service and rehabilitation to them.

299. HUNTER, David R., "Slums and Social Work," Child Welf., 41:9 (Nov. 1962), 387-393.
A discussion of how social work has not appreciated the significance of social class structure, and how psychological causation has been overemphasized in interpreting social problems. The author covers social work training, planning, and accountability.

300. HUNTINGTON FAMILY CENTER, INC., Multi-Service Project for Troubled Families in a Social Settlement Center in Syracuse, New York, Huntington Family Center, Inc., Syracuse, New York, 1961, 27 pp.
The Junior League supported a three-year multi-service project for troubled families (1958-1961). This document summarizes the

work, philosophy, and characteristics of the families of the project. During the first year, 33 families were treated by a combination of group work, casework, and community organization techniques. It is felt that long-term, acutely distressed, lower socio-economic families can be helped by such a concentrated effort. The second year saw 44 families receiving service. The report also contains five case summaries which illustrate the savings, in financial and human terms, to the community which invests concentrated help on these m.p. families.

301. LUKOFF, Irving, and MENCHER, Samuel, "A Critique of the Conceptual Foundation of Community Research Associates," *Social Service Review*, 36:4 (Dec. 1962), 443-444.
    The authors review the work of C.R.A. in a very thorough manner. The problem family definition is questioned, and the various approaches taken by C.R.A. in their research projects are sharply criticized. The techniques, research methodology, and evaluation techniques are all under fire.

302. MAHAFFEY, Maryann, "Serving Multi-Problem Families" (unpublished paper), Detroit, Michigan, 1961, 5 pp. (mimeo.).
    The author, who is program director of Brightmoor Community Center (Detroit), discusses changes which must be introduced in order to meet the needs of m.p. families. She suggests programs which can be introduced into Settlement Houses, and favours establishment of "District Social Service Centers" to eliminate a piecemeal approach to m.p. families.

303. PENNSYLVANIA (COMMONWEALTH OF), *Family Rehabilitation Program*, Department of Public Welfare, Office of Public Assistance, Harrisburg, Pennsylvania, 1962 (four county reports).

In 1961 Pennslyvania launched a pilot program in four counties under C.R.A. guidance, to determine the causes of dependence of Public Assistance families. An attempt will be made by casework and planned social services to restore families to possible self-dependency, and to prevent further social deterioration. The four county reports are: Indiana County (Apr. 1962, 71 pp.); Montgomery County (Mar. 1962, 25 pp.); Luzerne County (Apr. 1962, 36 pp.); Allegheny County (Aug. 1962, 40 pp.). Each report discusses the social and economic characteristics of Public Assistance families, and reviews preventative and rehabilitative potentialities.

304. UNIVERSITY OF KEELE, The Canford Families (monograph No. 6), The Sociological Review, Dec. 1962, 252 pp.
This is the sixth monograph published by the Department of Psychology of the University of Keele in Staffordshire, England. The report describes a five-year project which attempted to help 16 intact families who lived in an area of social disturbance, had a school child whose behaviour caused distress, and were not yet classified by any public authority as "problem families". The project used the reaching-out, preventative, family-centred type of social work approach, which included casework and group work methods. The family was approached as a "whole" rather than on the basis of individual problems. The eight contributors then go on to discuss in detail the families and the social work undertaken on their behalf.

305. YOUNG, Leontine, "Problem Parents," Ontario Welfare Reporter, 9:3 (Fall 1962), 1-9.
Speech given in Toronto to the Childrens' Aid Society annual meeting. The author traces the neglect and abuse of children today, and relates it to the isolation of the nuclear family. Examples are

given to illustrate her points. She issues a challenge to social workers to help structure family life.

306. LAMONT, Lois Goers, "An Analysis of a Project undertaken by Family Service of Jackson with Eighteen Multiple-Problem Families to Determine the Specific Needs of This Type of Family" (unpublished Master's thesis, School of Social Work, University of Michigan, 1957).

    An evaluation of the first 18 months of the co-operative project undertaken by 8 social agencies in Jackson County with 18 m.p. families. The study found that the social functioning of 70 per cent of the 16 families covered improved in at least one area. Five families showed no movement in any area, 11 families improved in at least one area, one improved in 6 of the 12 areas, while 4 families deteriorated in one area. The greatest change was the responsibility assumed by Family Service in maintaining contact with the family through extensive use of home calls. The greatest lack revealed by the study was co-ordinated planning which diminished as the project aged and Family Service assumed responsibility for the continuing treatment plans.

307. WHITE, Florence M., "The Multi-Problem Family and Mental Hospitalization," (unpublished Master's thesis, School of Social Work, University of Michigan, 1960).

    A study of 45 Washtenaw County families with children hospitalized at Ypsilanti State Hospital. Thirteen children from m.p. families and 14 from families with fewer problems are studied in relation to the way they come to the juvenile court prior to commitment to the State Hospital. In general, children from m.p. families tend to show disturbed behaviour at an earlier age than those from families with fewer problems.

APPENDIX A

BIBLIOGRAPHY December 1962 - April 1965

C A N A D A

308. ELKIN, Frederick, The Family in Canada, Canadian Conference on the Family, June 1964 (55 Parkdale Avenue, Ottawa 3, Ontario), 192 pp.
    Chapter 6 of this book deals with the atypical family in Canada, and discusses the m.p. family in the Canadian setting.

309. LAGEY, Joseph, and AYRES, Beverly, "Research on Multi-Problem Families," Soc. Worker, 32:1 (Jan.-Feb. 1964), 28-37.
    Summary of a survey of 117 action programs with m.p. families in North America. The types of approaches are analyzed, and recommendations are made for co-operation in research and information on the m.p. families.

310. LAIDLAW FOUNDATION, Summary of the Laidlaw Foundation Working Party on Multi-Problem Family Projects, Laidlaw Foundation, Dec. 1963 (50 Oak Street, Weston, Ontario), 9 pp.
    Highlights of a three-day conference held, under the auspices of the Laidlaw Foundation, to discuss m.p. projects in Vancouver, Winnipeg, London, Toronto, and Halifax. The Appendix includes a paper on Family Psychiatry by Dr. N. Epstein.

311. ONTARIO DEPARTMENT OF PUBLIC WELFARE, Long-Term Assistance Families - A Demonstration Project, Onatrio Department of Public Welfare, Jan. 1964 (Parliament Buildings, Toronto, Ontario), 39 pp.
    The 200 "long-term assistance" families chosen for this project were divided equally into a control and a study group. In a 6-

month period the 100 study cases, all on public welfare, received intensive service from a social worker. The results indicated that concentrated attention given to these families brought about significant improvements.

312. ---------, Hamilton Demonstration Project, Ontario Department of Public Welfare, Nov. 1964, 18 pp.
    A second project with "long-term assistance" families (see reference #311). Of the 100 cases given special attention for six months, 56 left the relief rolls and 36 heads of families obtained employment, which was a much higher percentage than in the control group of 100 families. Case illustrations are given to show how progress was achieved.

313. SCHLESINGER, Benjamin, "Programmes d'action pour les familles inadaptées," Service Social, 13:1 (Jan.-June 1964), 88-103 (published by Laval University, Quebec).
    Paper, prepared for the Conference on "Socially Handicapped Families", which covers the approaches to m.p. families in North America and Europe and the social-psychological factors related to m.p. families.

314. WEISS, Abe, Current Psychiatric Family Investigation: Theory and Research, Canadian Conference on the Family, June 1964 (55 Parkdale Avenue, Ottawa 3, Ontario), 100 pp. (mimeo.).
    This document reviews in detail selected studies relating to psychiatric investigation of families under the headings Family Life and Mental Illness, Psychotherapy and the Family, and Methods of Family Study.

F R A N C E

315. AIDE À TOUTE DÉTRESSE, Nouveaux aspects de la famille, Aide à Toute Détresse, Paris, 1964, 125 pp.

The third in a series of monographs (see references #294, 295) on problem families in France. This report analyzes the socialization, adaptation, and deviance of the families. A discussion of mental health is also included. The two principal authors of this monograph are Jean Labbens and Christian Debuyst.

316. UNESCO, Conference on Socially Handicapped Families, Paris, Feb. 1964 (papers available from: Bureau de Recherches Sociales, 53 rue de la Fontaine-au-Roi, Paris 11^e).

An international conference whose 250 members came from eight West European countries, South Africa, Brazil, Lebanon, Canada, and the United States. The participants ranged from architects to sociologists, and from jurists and lawyers to social workers, the latter composing about half the membership. The medical profession, including psychiatry, was well represented. The three-day program was divided into three main areas: (1) Poverty and Society; (2) Poverty and Socially Handicapped Families; and (3) Action and Research for Socially Handicapped Families. Plenary sessions heard papers on Poverty and on Community Development by Peter Townsend of Britain; Vilhelm Aubert of Norway; Andre Tunc, law professor from Paris; Christian Debuyst, Belgian psychologist; and Lloyd Ohlin of Columbia University. Dr. Otto Klineberg, social psychologist at the Sorbonne, led a panel discussion on problem families. The conference was organized also into five working parties of about 15 members each, who shared knowledge in their respective fields.

UNITED STATES

317. CURTIS, James L., SIMON, Melly, BOYKIN, Frances L., and NOE, Emma R., "Observations on 29 Multi-Problem Families,"

Amer. J. Orthopsychiat., 34:3 (Apr. 1964), 510-517.

The 29 families, predominantly Negro, were serviced by the Salvation Army Service Bureau in New York for an average duration of 5 years. The treatment approach was of a supportive, directive, re-educational casework type. Two-thirds of the families were fatherless or were living in common-law union. The paper describes the characteristics of these m.p. families and the treatment results.

318. GEISMAR, L. L. and LA SORTE, Michael A., Understanding the Multi-Problem Family, New York: Association Press, 1964 (291 Broadway, New York, New York 10007), 224 pp.

An attempt to present a scientific framework for analyzing and classifying the m.p. family. The sample studied consisted of 75 families located in a New Haven, Connecticut, Neighborhood Improvement scheme. The method is based on the "Profile of Family Functioning", refined after its use in the St. Paul studies. An attempt was made to distinguish between "stable" and "problem" families through the use of the profile. The sample divided about equally into these two categories. The profile, presented in the appendix of the book, is an assessment of inter- and intra-personal relationships of the family members in various areas of their life experiences.

319. MEYER, Carol, "Individualizing the Multi-Problem Family," Soc. Casewk., 44:5 (May 1963), 267-272.

The author, who feels that the term m.p. family is appropriate, describes characteristics of this type of family and relates their situation to poverty. She also discusses the techniques of helping through the "reaching out" concept.

320. NATIONAL FEDERATION OF SETTLEMENTS AND NEIGHBORHOOD CENTERS, Neighborhood Centers Serve the Troubled Family, National Federation of Settlements and Neighborhood Centers, Chicago, Illinois, 1964, 113 pp.
   A report of a conference held in March 1964. The three major papers by Marion Craine, Leonard Schneiderman, and Joseph Lagey discuss the m.p. family as a challenge to the profession, some methodological problems, and research questions. The report also includes a summary of 12 projects dealing with m.p. families.

321. WILLIE, Charles V., WAGENFIELD, Morton O., and CARY, Lee J., "Patterns of Rent Payment among Problem Families," Soc. Casewk., 45:8 (Oct. 1964), 465-471.
   The role of the social worker as "intercessor" between the families in arrears and the Housing Authority in a Syracuse low-rent housing unit is explained and the usefulness of a social worker in relating the problem families to the various civic authorities and outside social agencies is stressed.

322. WILLIE, Charles V., and WEINANDY, Janet, "The Structure and Composition of 'Problem' and 'Stable' Families in a Low-Income Population," Marr. Fam. Living, 25:4 (Nov. 1963), 439-447.
   Description of the similarities and differences between two samples of tenants in a Syracuse low-rent public housing project. The authors plead for techniques other than social casework in working with problem families.

ADDRESSES

(J) = Journal

Australia
Victorian Council of Social Service, 495 Collins Street, Melbourne C.I.

Britain
British (The) Journal of Delinquency (J), 8 Bourdon Street, Davies Street, London W.1.
British Journal of Psychiatric Social Work (J), 1 Park Crescent, London W.1.
British Journal of Sociology (J), Routledge and Kegan Paul, Broadway House, 68-74 Carter Lane, London E.C.4.
British Medical Journal (J), Tavistock Square, London W.C.1.
Burgh Factor -- see Housing Authority below.
Canadian Welfare (J) -- see Canada.
Case Conference (J), 57 Mayfield Road, Sanderstead, Surrey.
Crowley House, Middlemore Homes, Weoley Park Road, Selly Oak, Birmingham 29.
Eugenics Quarterly (J), Eugenics Society, 69 Eccleston Square, London S.W.1.
Faber and Faber Ltd., 24 Russell Square, London W.C.1.
Family Service Units, 207 Marylebone Road, London N.W.1.
George Allen and Unwin Ltd., 40 Museum Street, London W.C.1.
Her Majesty's Stationery Office -- check with United Kingdom Information Service nearest to you.
Housing (J), Institute of Housing, 50 Tufton Street, Westminster, London S.W.1.
Housing Authority, Burgh Factor, Paisley, Scotland.
Housing Newsletter (J) -- see Canada.
Institute (The) of Housing, 50 Tufton Street, Westminster, London S.W.1.
Institute for the Study and Treatment of Delinquency, 8 Bourdon Street, Davies Street, London W.1.
Joint University Council for Social Studies and Public Administration, c/o Willmer Brothers

and Company Ltd., 62-68 Chester Street, Birkenhead.
Journal of Housing (J) -- see United States.
Lancet (J), Lancet Ltd., 7 Adam Street, Adelphi, London W.C.2.
London County Council, Public Health Department, The County Hall, Westminster Bridge, London S.E.1.
Macmillan and Company Ltd., 10 St. Martin's Street, London W.C.2.
Magistrate (The) (J), Tavistock House South, Tavistock Square, London W.C.1.
Medical (The) Officer (J), 72-78 Fleet Street, London E.C.4.
Middlemore Homes, Weoley Park Road, Selly Oak, Birmingham 29.
Pacifist Service Units, 56 Grove Street, Liverpool 7.
Public Health (J), Bailliere, Tindall and Cox, 7 Hennrietta Street, London W.C.2.
Quarterly Review (J), 50 Albemale Street, London W.1.
Routledge and Kegan Paul, Broadway House, 68-74 Carter Lane, London E.C.4.
Rotterdam Social Welfare Department -- see Holland.
Royal Society of Health Journal (J), 90 Buckingham Palace Road, London S.W.1.
Social Service (J), National Council of Social Service, 26 Bedford Square, London W.C.1.
Social Work (J), Denison House, 296 Vauxhall Bridge Road, London S.W.1.
Squire Law Library, Old Schools, Cambridge.
Tavistock Publications Ltd., 11 New Fetter Lane, London E.C.4.
University of Cambridge, Department of Criminal Science, Faculty of Law, Cambridge.
University of Toronto Press -- see Canada.

Canada

Canadian Conference on Social Work, 55 Parkdale Avenue, Ottawa 3, Ontario.
Canadian Welfare (J), 55 Parkdale Avenue, Ottawa 3, Ontario.
Canadian Welfare Council, 55 Parkdale Avenue, Ottawa 3, Ontario.
Community Chest and Councils of the Greater Vancouver Area, 1625 West 8th Avenue, Vancouver 9,

British Columbia.
Congdon, H. S., County Building, Walkerton, Ontario.
Family Service Agency of Greater Vancouver, 1637 W. 8th Avenue, Vancouver 9, British Columbia.
Globe and Mail (newspaper), 140 King Street W., Toronto, Ontario.
Housing Authority of Metropolitan Toronto, 415 Gerrard Street E., Toronto 2, Ontario.
Housing Newsletter (J), 454 University Avenue, Toronto, Ontario.
Journal of the Ontario Children's Aid Societies (J), 570 Water Street, Peterborough, Ontario.
Laidlaw Foundation, 150 Eglinton Avenue E., Toronto 12, Ontario.
Macleans (J), Maclean-Hunter Publishing Company Ltd., 481 University Avenue, Toronto, Ontario.
Ontario Welfare Council, 96 Bloor Street W., Toronto 5, Ontario.
Ontario Welfare Reporter (J), 96 Bloor Street W., Toronto 5, Ontario.
Social Planning Council of Metropolitan Toronto, 160 Bay Street, Toronto, Ontario.
Social Worker (J), 18 Rideau Street, Ottawa, Ontario.
United Community Services of London, 224 Central Avenue, London, Ontario.
University of British Columbia, School of Social Work, Vancouver 8, British Columbia.
University of Toronto, School of Social Work, Toronto 5, Ontario.
University of Toronto Press, Front Campus, University of Toronto, Toronto 5, Ontario.
Vancouver Community Chest and Councils, 1625 West 8th Avenue, Vancouver 9, British Columbia.
Welfare Council of Greater Windsor, 1590 Ouellette Avenue, Windsor, Ontario.
Welfare Council of Ottawa, 329 Chapel Street, Ottawa 3, Ontario.

France
Aide à Toute Détresse, 53 rue de la Fontaine-au-Roi, Paris 11e.

Holland
Case Conference (J) -- see Britain.
Magistrate (The) (J) -- see Britain.
Medical (The) Officer (J) -- see Britain.

Ministry for Social Work, 7 Binnenhof, The Hague.
Public Health (J) -- see Britain.
Quarterly Review (J) -- see Britain.
Rotterdam Municipal Welfare Department, Rotterdam.
Staats drukkerij, Fluweles Burgwal 18, Gravenhage, The Hague.

United States
Adult Leadership (J) 743 N. Wabash Avenue, Chicago 11, Illinois.
Alameda County Council on Social Planning, 337-- 13th Street, Oakland 12, California.
American Journal of Orthopsychiatry (J), 1790 Broadway, New York 19, New York.
American Journal of Public Health (J), 1790 Broadway, New York 19, New York.
American Public Welfare Association, 1313 E. 60th Street, Chicago 37, Illinois.
Baden Street Settlement, 152 Baden Street, Rochester 5, New York.
Brooklyn Bureau of Social Service, 285 Schermerhorn Street, Brooklyn, New York.
Brubaker, Susan (Miss), 2416 Waverly Street, Philadelphia 46, Pennsylvania.
Chemung County Department of Public Welfare, Elmira, New York.
Child Welfare (J), 44 E. 23rd Street, New York 10, New York.
Children (J), Children's Bureau, Department of Health, Education, and Welfare, Washington 25, D.C.
Citizens Housing and Planning Council of New York, 20 W. 40th Street, New York 18, New York.
Colorado State Department of Welfare, State Services Building, Denver 3, Colorado.
Columbia University Press, 2960 Broadway, New York 27, New York.
Community Chest and Council Inc. of Greater St. Paul, 400 Wilder Bldg., St. Paul 2, Minnesota.
Community Council of the Atlanta Area, 626 Candler Building, Atlanta 3, Georgia.
Community Council of Greater New York, 345 E. 34th Street, New York 17, New York.
Community Research Associates, 124 E. 40th Street, New York 16, New York.
Community Welfare Council of Greater Milwaukee, Milwaukee, Wisconsin.

Council of Social Agencies of Rochester and Munroe County, 70 N. Water Street, Rochester 4, New York.
Council of Social Planning of Berkeley, P.O. Box 769, Berkeley 1, California.
Council on Social Work Education, 345 E. 46th Street, New York 17, New York.
Douglas County Welfare Administration, Omaha, Nebraska.
Family Service Association of America, 215 Park Avenue S., New York 3, New York.
Family Service Association of Indianapolis, 615 N. Alabama Street, Indianapolis 4, Indiana.
Family Service Highlights (J), 44 E. 23rd Street, New York 10, New York.
Family Service of Oakland County, United Community Services of Metropolitan Detroit, 51 Warren Avenue W., Detroit 1, Michigan.
Geismar, Ludwig L., School of Social Work, Rutgers State University, New Brunswick, New Jersey.
Golden Anniversary White House Conference on Children and Youth, c/o Columbia University Press, 2960 Broadway, New York 27, New York.
Grant Foundation, 1441 Broadway, New York, New York.
Greenleigh Associates, 437 Fifth Avenue, New York, New York.
Health and Welfare Council of the Baltimore Area, Inc., 22 Light Street, Baltimore 3, Maryland.
Housing Authority of Baltimore City, 10 N. Calvert Street, Baltimore 3, Maryland.
Illinois Public Aid Commission, Room 2000, 160 N. La Salle Street, Chicago 1, Illinois.
Interdepartmental Neighborhood Service Center, Office of the Mayor, 145 W. 125th Street, New York 27, New York.
Journal for Study of Interpersonal Processes (J), 1610 New Hampshire Avenue N.W., Washington 9, D.C.
Journal of American Academy of Child Psychiatry (J), International University Press, 227 W. 13th Street, New York 11, New York.
Journal of Consulting Psychology (J), 1333--16th Street N.W., Washington, D.C.
Journal of Housing (J), 1413 K Street N.W., Washington 5, D.C.

Journal of Nervous and Mental Disease (J), 428 E. Preston Street, Baltimore, Maryland.
Journal of Social Work Process (J), University of Pennsylvania Press, Philadelphia, Pennsylvania.
Lee, Dr. Rose Hum, 3014 E. Wetherfield Road, Phoenix 22, Arizona.
Library (The) Counselor (J), Colorado State Department of Public Welfare, State Services Building, Denver 3, Colorado.
Louisiana Department of Public Welfare, New Orleans, Louisiana.
Louisiana State University, School of Social Welfare, Baton Rouge 3, Louisiana.
Marriage and Family Living (J), 1219 University Avenue S.E., Minneapolis 14, Minnesota.
Mendell, Dr. David, The Medical Towers, Houston, Texas.
Mental Hygiene (J), 10 Columbus Circle, New York 19, New York.
Milwaukee (City of), 2921 N. 2nd Street, Milwaukee 12, Wisconsin (Attention Mr. Frank P. Zeidler).
National Association of Housing and Redevelopment Officials (NAHRO), 1413 K Street N.W., Washington 5, D.C.
National Federation of Settlements and Neighborhood Centers, 226 W. 47th Street, New York 36, New York.
National Institute of Mental Health, Community Services Branch, Robin Building, Room 3A-02, 7981 Eastern Avenue, Silver Spring, Maryland.
New York City Chapter, National Association of Social Workers, 14 E. 28th Street, New York 16, New York.
New York City Department of Public Welfare, 250 Church Street, New York 13, New York.
New York City Youth Board, 79 Madison Avenue, New York 16, New York.
New York State Charities Aid Association, 105 E. 22nd Street, New York 10, New York.
Philadelphia School District, Andrew Jackson School, 12th and Federal Street, Philadelphia 47, Pennsylvania.
Pittsburgh Department of Public Welfare, Pittsburgh, Pennsylvania.
Pubic Aid in Illinois (J), Room 2000, 160 N. La

Salle Street, Chicago 1, Illinois.
Public Welfare (J), 1313 E. 60th Street, Chicago 37, Illinois.
Rand McNally and Company, 405 Park Avenue, New York 22, New York.
San Mateo County Superintendent of Schools, 538 Jefferson Avenue, Redwood City, California.
Social Casework (J), 44 E. 23rd Street, New York 10, New York.
Social Service Review (J), University of Chicago, Chicago 37, Illinois.
Social Work (J), 95 Madison Avenue, New York 16, New York.
State Charities Aid Association -- see New York State Charities Aid Association.
State University of Iowa, Iowa City, Iowa.
Survey Midmonthly (J), 112 E. 19th Street, New York 3, New York.
Syracuse University Youth Development Center, Syracuse 10, New York.
Texas (State of), Department of Health, Austin, Texas.
Tucker, Dorothy (Miss), c/o Grant County Guidance Center, Room 4, Bayley Block, Platteville, Wisconsin.
United Community Council of Columbus, 137 East State Street, Columbus 15, Ohio.
United Community Funds and Councils of America, 345 E. 46th Street, New York 17, New York.
United Community Services of Metropolitan Boston, Mason Memorial Building, 14 Somerset Street, Boston 8, Massachusetts.
United Community Services of Omaha, 726 Kilpatrick Building, Omaha 2, Nebraska.
United South End Settlements, 20 Union Park, Boston 18, Massachusetts.
University of Minnesota Family Study Center, Minneapolis 14, Minnesota.
Washtenaw County Department of Social Welfare, Room 132, County Building, Ann Arbor, Michigan.
Welfare Council of Erie, Erie, Pennsylvania.
Welfare Council of Metropolitan Chicago, 123 W. Madison Street, Chicago 2, Illinois.
Youth Conservation Services, Department of Welfare, Room 507, City Hall Annex, Philadelphia 7, Pennsylvania.

Youth Development Center -- see Syracuse University Youth Development Center.

Miscellaneous
Aide à Toute Détresse -- see France.
Centre d'Étude sur la Delinquance Juvenile, 49 Rue Chatelain, Brussels 5.
Child Welfare (J) -- see United States.
Ontario Welfare Reporter (J) -- see Canada.

AUTHOR INDEX

(Numbers refer to listings in Bibliography)

A.R.H.F. 3
Ackerman, N.W. 109
Aide à Toute Détresse
  294,295,315
Alameda County Welfare
  Department 98
Allegheny County Board
  of Assistance 99
Allin, K.D. 54
Austin, D. 100
Axelrod, S.J. 235
Ayres, B. 55,68,101,
  169,170,171,172,
  174,309

Baden Street Settlement
  102,103,104,105
Baker, M.S. 106
Baldamus, W. 4
Barbour, H.S. 107,108
Barclay, I.T. 5
Bargans, R. 175
Bastiaans, J. 6
Baughn, B. 107,108
Becker, J. 56
Behrens, M.L. 109
Beisser, P.T. 110,130
Bemmels, V.G. 111
Bender, A. 112
Berg, M.F. 113
Bernard, S.E. 137
Birt, C.J. 114,115
Bishop, A.J. 116
Blacker, C.P. (ed.) 7
Bodman, F. 8
Booth, C. 9
Boykin, F.L. 317
Bradley, E. 57
Bradshaw, D. 117
Brickman, L. 118

Briskin, S.I. 10
Browne, A. 119,120
Brubaker, S. 121
Bryant, C.B. 122
Buck, C. 123
Buell, B. 123,124,125,
  126,127,128,130,153,
  280
Buell, B., and Associ-
  ates 129
Bureau de Recherches
  Sociales 85
Burgess, E.W. 131
Burgess, I.L. 87

Cameron, E. 58
Caplan, G. 238
Cary, L.J. 208,291,321
Case Conference 132
Charen, S. 133
Chatterjee, P. 58
Chemung County Depart-
  ment of Public Welfare
  134
Cheow, J. 59
Christensen, H. (ed.)
  135
Clark, I. 136
Cohen, W. 137
Colorado State Depart-
  ment of Welfare 138
Community Chests and
  Councils of the
  Greater Vancouver
  Area 60,61
Community Council of
  Greater New York 141
Community Council of the
  Atlanta Area 139,140
Community Research Asso-
  ciates 142,143

Community Services Center 144
Community Welfare Council of Greater Milwaukee 145
Compton, B.R. 146,147
Congdon, H.S. 62
Conlan, M. 148
Cookson, J.S. 11
Coombe, D.L. 63
Council on Social Work Education 149
Crawford, F.R. 150
Curtis, J.L. 317

Debuyst, R.G. 296
Dennis, N. 41
Dick, K. 151
Donnison, D. 12
Douglas County Welfare Administration 152

Edmison, E. 58
Elkin, F. 308
Eller, G.C. 153
Erie Welfare Council 154

Family Centered Project (Staff of) 261
Family Service Agency of Greater Vancouver 64
Family Service Association of Indianapolis 155
Family Service Units 13
Fantl, B. 156,157,158
Feider, L.J. 176
Fike, N. 159
Fisher, G. 107,108
Fisher, S. 160,161,162
Fossier, M. 163
Furness, A. 65

Geismar, L.L. 164,165,166,167,168,169,170,171,172,173,174,318

Gendron, P. 59
Gideon, H.J. 175
Glabe, D.B. 176
Grant Foundation 177
Greenleigh Associates 297,298
Grunwold, H. 178,179

Haas, W. 180
Hallinan, H. 181
Harris, W. 107,108
Hartman, S.S. 183
Hatcher, G.H. 153
Hawarth, E. 182
Health and Welfare Council of the Baltimore Area 184
Henry, C.S. 185
Hill, R. 186
Hillman, A. 187,188
Hobman, D.L. 88
Hoffman, W. 189
Hommann, M.S. 190,191
Horsham, B. 59
Hunter, D.R. 299
Huntington Family Center Inc. 300
Hurwitz, J.I. 264

Idelson, R. 264
Institute for the Study and Treatment of Delinquency 14
Institute of Housing 15
Irvine, E.E. 16,17
Ish, J.G. 192

Joint Family Services Project 66
Joint University Council for Social Studies and Public Administration, England 18
Jones, D.C. 19
Jones, D. 20,21

Journal of Housing 193, 194

Kandle, R.P. 123
Kasius, C. 195
Kaufman, I. 242
Keith, A.M. 67
Kern, M.R. 237
Koos, E.L. 196

Lagey, J.C. 55,68,309
Laidlaw Foundation 310
Lamont, L.G. 306
Lampkin, L. 197
La Sorte, M.A. 173,174, 318
Lassell, M. 22
Leader, A. 198
Lee, R.H. 199
Lewis, H. 200
Liebenberg, B. 133
Lindenberg, R.E. 201
Lippman, H.S. 202
London County Council 23
Love, S. 203
Lukoff, I. 301

M.L.D. 27
Mahaffey, M. 302
Marcuse, B. 70,71
Mayer, H. 203
McCarthy, H.L. 204
McClary, H.C. 205
McDowell, J. 206
McEachern, W.D.C. 69
McKay, S. 45
McKibbon, B. 207,208
McLain, O. 209
Meier, G. 210
Mencher, S. 300
Mendell, D. 160,161,162
Meyer, C. 319
Middlemore Homes 24,25
Mill, J. van 89
Miller, W.B. 211

Milwaukee (City of) 212
Ministry for Social Work 90,91,92,93
Ministry of Housing 26
Minnesota State Welfare Conference 213

NAHRO (National Association of Housing and Redevelopment Officials) 214,215
National Federation of Settlements and Neighborhood Centers 320
Neuhaus, R. 216
New Haven Council of Social Agencies 217
New York City Chapter National Association of Social Workers 218
New York City Youth Board 219,220
New York State Charities Aid Association 221,222
Noe, E.R. 317
Noles, J.D. 223
Norman, F.M. 224

Ojemann, R.H. (ed.) 225
Ontario Department of Public Welfare 311,312
Oppenheimer, H. 226
Ormsby, R. 227
Overton, A. 228,229,230, 231,232,233

Page, H.O. 176,234,235
Page, M.O. 236
Paget, N. 237
Parad, H.J. 238
Pennsylvania (Commonwealth of) 303
Philadelphia Public Welfare Department 239

Philp, A.F. 28,29
Podell, L. 197
Pyrke, M. 256

Querido, A. 94

Racine, A. 296
Rappaport, M.F. 240
Regensberg, J. 241
Reiner, B.S. 242
Roach, J. 243
Robinson, J. 58
Robinson, M.O. 72,244, 245
Robinson, R. 246
Rochester and Munroe County Council of Social Agencies 247, 248
Rogers, M.N. 249
Roney, J.L. 250
Roseman, R. 73
Rowan, C.T. 251

Samuels, G. 252,253,254
Savage, S.W. 30,31
Scheidlinger, S. 255, 256
Scherz, F. 257
Schlesinger, B. 74,75, 76,313
Scott, B. 77
Scott, J.A. 32,33
Sharpe, M. 58
Shereshefsky, P.M. 133
Sheridan, M.D. 34,35, 95,96
Sherman, S.N. 258
Silverman, A.D. 36,37
Simon, M. 317
Simmons, H.E. 259
Smith, J. 284
Smith, M.A. 38,39,40
Soyer, D. 260
Spencer, J.C. 41,77

Spurgin, C. 97
Stallybrass, C.O. 42
Star, J. 262
Stephens, T. (ed.) 43
Stinson, M. 263
Stone, E. 264
Straus, M.A. 265
Strickler, E. 266
Strnad, L. 151
Svihus, R.H. 267
Syracuse University 268

Terresberry, S. 269
Thomson, D. 78
Timms, N. 4,28,44
Tinker, K.H. 233,270, 271,272
Tucker, D. 273
Tuxford, J. 41

Unesco 316
United Community Council of Columbus 274
United Community Funds and Councils of America 275,276
United Community Services (London, Ontario) 79,80
United Community Services of Boston 277, 278
University of Keele 304

Van Vleet, P.P. 110
Veitch, B. 59
Victorian Council of Social Service 1,2
Voiland, A.L. 279,280
Voiland, A.L., and Associates 281

Wagenfeld, M.O. 291,321
Wagner, N.N. 282
Walker, G. 283

Ward, H.P. 133
Warham, J. 45
Warner, R.L. 284
Watson, E. 65
Wedemeyer, J.M. 130
Weinandy, J.E. 285,322
Weiss, A. 314
Weiss, D. 81
Welfare Council of
  Greater Windsor 82
Welfare Council of
  Metropolitan Chicago
  286,287
Welfare Council of
  Ottawa, 83,84
Whale, M. 288

Whelan, R. 289
White, F.M. 307
Willie, C.V. 290,291,
  321,322
Willson, F.M.G. 46
Wilson, H.C. 47,48,49
Wiltse, K. 292
Wofinden, R.C. 50,51
Wood, E. 293
Woodhouse, D.L. 52
Wresinski, l'Abbé J. 86

Young, L. 305
Younghusband, E.L. 53

Zilbach, J.J. 264

www.ingramcontent.com/pod-product-compliance
Lightning Source LLC
Chambersburg PA
CBHW020254030426
42336CB00010B/758